PRAISE FOR *ZERO LIMITS LIVING*

"I've watched Dr. Joe's evolution as a leading-edge author for decades. His latest book is a breakthrough in personal development and spirituality. It's truly a new map to success. I loved it."

—MARCI SHIMOFF, #1 *NEW YORK TIMES* BESTSELLING

AUTHOR, *HAPPY FOR NO REASON*

"An eye-opener! We need this book now more than ever before. It's empowering, enlightening, and entertaining too!"

—LEE MILTEER, AUTHOR, SPEAKER, AND BUSINESS COACH

"If you're seeking a path to a limitless existence, I highly recommend *Zero Limits Living* by Dr. Joe Vitale, unquestionably one of the greatest self-help authors of our time."

- MOE ROCK, PUBLISHER, MUSIC PRODUCER, AND

BESTSELLING AUTHOR, *THE MORAL COMPASS*

"These high-consciousness techniques include understanding the Universe conspires to help us, harnessing the power of the collective unconscious, identifying with our inner 'I' of divinity, rewiring our brains, and turning any failure into feedback on our way to our dreams. Welcome to living a life of infinite possibilities!"

—DR. TASSEL FAITH SHANEBROOK, FOUNDER, YOU ARE YOUR OWN HERO

"Empowering and transformative, this isn't your ordinary self-help book! This masterpiece is the only book you will ever need to unlock the secrets of attracting your desires and goals with precision and grace. Its profound wisdom not only reveals the path to achieving your dreams, but also bestows the gift of inner peace, nurturing a serene mind and soul amidst life's chaos. With the three-part formula, prepare to kick limiting beliefs to the curb and finally have a limitless life!"

—AMBERLY LAGO, BESTSELLING AUTHOR, HOST, *TRUE GRIT AND GRACE* PODCAST, MINDSET COACH, AND TEDX SPEAKER

"A brilliant synthesis of spirituality and self-help, revealing a new system for getting results in a balanced, healthy, and accelerated way. I highly recommend this amazing book."

—MARY MORRISSEY, AUTHOR, *BRAVE THINKING*, AND FOUNDER, BRAVE THINKING INSTITUTE

"Dr. Joe's use of his own compelling story will have you captivated, inspired, and ready to break down limitations in order to live the life you deserve."

—DARIUSH SOUDI, FOUNDER, GLADIATOR MASTERY

"Reading Dr. Joe Vitale's latest book, *Zero Limits Living*, will be the difference between talking about the results you want to see in your life and actually achieving them! Read the book, do the work, reap the rewards!"

—CLARISSA BURT, AUTHOR, *THE SELF-ESTEEM REGIME*

ZERO LIMITS LIVING

ALSO BY JOE VITALE

ZERO LIMITS LIVING

The Three Essential Pillars to Achieving All Your Life's Goals

DR. JOE VITALE

Matt Holt Books
An Imprint of BenBella Books, Inc.
Dallas, TX

Zero Limits Living copyright © 2024 by Hypnotic Marketing Inc.

Matt Holt is an imprint of BenBella Books, Inc.
10440 N. Central Expressway
Suite 800
Dallas, TX 75231
benbellabooks.com
Send feedback to feedback@benbellabooks.com

BenBella and *Matt Holt* are federally registered trademarks.

Printed in the United States of America
10 9 8 7 6 5 4 3 2 1

Library of Congress Control Number: 2023036381
ISBN 9781637744963 (hardcover)
ISBN 9781637744970 (electronic)

Copyediting by James Fraleigh
Proofreading by Michael Fedison and Cape Cod Compositors, Inc.
Text design and composition by Aaron Edmiston
Cover design and illustration by Brigid Pearson
Printed by Lake Book Manufacturing

Special discounts for bulk sales are available.
Please contact bulkorders@benbellabooks.com.

For the "I" within you.

CONTENTS

We are not human beings having a spiritual experience.
We are spiritual beings having a human experience.

—PIERRE TEILHARD DE CHARDIN

PROLOGUE

No matter who you are, where you are, or what challenge you are facing right now, I have good news for you.

I know what it's like to struggle.

And I know what it's like to succeed.

If you let me, I can help you.

Will you?

Let me explain.

At the end of 2021—while the world was still in a pandemic, and as I was recovering from an agonizing three-year divorce, developing a new relationship, dealing with the deaths of family members and best friends, and learning to move all my business online—I had a breakthrough.

It was an "illumination" that brought together my entire life experience in self-help and metaphysics, spirituality, and practicality. Everything came together in one flash of insight that became what I ended up calling "zero limits living."

I shared it with my business advisor at the time, Sean Donahoe. He loved it. He saw the wisdom of it. Together we delivered the new material online. We invited a small audience, turned people away to keep it informal, and wowed those who attended.

We recorded the event and transcribed it, and I transformed it into this book. I've done my best to make this material easy—accessible to anyone—and designed it to help you do one thing: get results. Not just material accomplishments but also spiritual awakening. It's time for a win-win of the highest level possible.

This three-part program can help you in numerous ways. The "three pillars" of this breakthrough method are designed to get you through whatever you are dealing with right now, and then go beyond it. This is no airy-fairy "woo woo." I am a practical man. If something I try doesn't get real-world results, then I'm not interested.

After all, I was homeless in the late 1970s. I was in poverty for most of the 1980s. I know struggle, strain, worry, and strife. But I've also gone beyond them. Since then, I've written more than eighty books, recorded more than fifteen music albums, appeared in more than seventeen movies, created more than two hundred products, originated a famous coaching program, and traveled the entire planet as a speaker, delivering this message of practical spirituality on stages worldwide.

I also have my own online television show, *Zero Limits Living*, and a podcast, *Zero Limits*, and am currently completing a movie, also titled *Zero Limits*. Perhaps you notice a theme here.

The message I convey through all this material not only works; it can transform you into a being that knows how to attract magic and miracles, and routinely achieve goals big and small—all while living a more serene life.

And now I want to share it with you.

If you are holding this book, you are obviously open enough to consider a new way of living. If you can remain open as you read, I will deliver a message of both hope and method. I will show you how to have, do, or be virtually anything you desire. I know you've heard the promise before. This time, you'll get it. I'll deliver it. Today. In this very book.

The reason I can make this promise to you is this: I read the other books, too. When I was homeless or in poverty, I went to the library. I devoured the success literature of the world. But I didn't change. Not fast enough, anyway. I'd read, for instance, Napoleon Hill's *Think and Grow Rich* and wonder why I wasn't rich after it. What was missing in the book? What was wrong with me?

Nothing was wrong with me.

Nothing is wrong with you, either.

I discovered that even the classics are missing some elements. I still love self-help books and their legendary authors, from Dale Carnegie to Claude Bristol. But I discovered that if you don't know and apply the elements those authors didn't know at the time they were living, then you may not have the results you want and deserve.

This book explains the three pillars you need. The problem facing previous self-help authors was that they focused on one pillar, at best two, but never three. They didn't because they couldn't. They didn't have (as we say in Texas) "the whole enchilada." This book is the whole meal. Call it a three-course dinner. Call it balanced nutrition. Either way, this is your ticket to a whole new world.

Ready or not, here we go . . .

You are not a drop in the ocean.
You are the entire ocean in a drop.

—RUMI

ZERO LIMITS LIVING SYMPHONY

Dr. Joe Vitale

In the lands of time and tide, where moments twist and
   sway,
Lies a tale of choice and chance, a dance of night and day.
A life of spontaneity, a path that's all its own,
Where every step's a mystery, and every breeze unknown.

Yet in this land of chaos, of unpredictability,
There lies a deeper secret, a truth that sets us free.
For in each fleeting moment, with every choice we make,
We seize the reins of destiny, and forge the path we take.

The sun that greets the morning, the stars that grace the
    night,
Are guides upon our journey, as we navigate through life.
Embrace the sweet uncertainty, the joys of serendipity,
For life is but a canvas, and we are its artistry.

To live a life of spontaneity, to let our hearts be light,
To dance upon the winds of chance, and sail into the night,
We mustn't fear the unknown, nor be shackled by the past,
For it's within the present that our futures shall be cast.

And as we stride through realms untamed, our spirits wild
    and free,
We'll find that every moment is an opportunity,
To write our own adventure, to seize our fate and hold,
A life of boundless freedom, where the story's yet untold.

So let us dance in moonlit skies, and sing with morning
    birds,
For every note and every step, we'll lead a life undeterred.
In spontaneity, we'll soar, in actions, we'll direct,
A symphony of zero limits living, where our dreams and
    fate connect.

Introduction

MY THUNDERBOLT

You've probably never been struck by lightning. Good thing, as you most likely wouldn't have survived. But what if the lightning bolt was inspiration? And what if, instead of frying you, it awakened you?

That's what happened to me.

Let me explain.

I meditate a lot. Daily. I use everything from Ho'oponopono (which I'll explain later) to Zen to other Buddhist meditations to my own Witness Meditation. I also sit in the hot tub almost every night, under the Texas sky, and look at each twinkling star and say, "Thank you."

Through all of the inner exploration that I do, occasionally something will inspire me. And those insights lead to books, songs, articles, products—any number of things. But recently, this thunderbolt of an enlightening experience came through on a sweeping level: not only did it go down my spine and awaken all of my chakras (energy centers), but it pulled together everything I have done in my entire life.

Now, you may know me as the "law of attraction guy" who was in the hit movie *The Secret,* or the Ho'oponopono guy who started an avid following with my book *Zero Limits.* Maybe you go all the way back and know that I was practicing marketing and copywriting in the early 1990s and wrote books like *Hypnotic Writing* and *Buying Trances.* You also may know that I learned how to bend horseshoes by hand and wrote a book about it, called *Anything Is Possible.* Or maybe you heard I re-created myself as a musician at age sixty and have recorded several albums before I turned seventy years old. Wrote a book about that, too, with Jaime Vendera, called *Mind over Music.*

I've written extensively about what I learned from all these different areas, but these books all have been slices of life—separate subject categories. Thus far I hadn't crafted anything that could pull them all together. There wasn't one formula that synthesized it all.

Not until lightning struck.

But then this enlightening experience took place and I had the "aha!" The skies opened. God spoke. My mind melted. I had an insight, an *afflatus,* as the Roman consul and writer Cicero might say, which pulled it all together. It led to my sketching a graphic that was pregnant with meaning.

Here's the image I composed.

THE 3 PILLARS
The Art & Science of Zero Limits Living

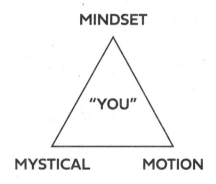

MINDSET

"YOU"

MYSTICAL   **MOTION**

MINDSET	MYSTICAL	MOTION
• Paradigms	• "I" of You	• Inspired Action
• Intentions/ Counterintentions	• Asking/Receiving	• Continuous Action
• Brain Hacks	• Awakening	• Refined Action

What came to me first was the "You" in the middle of the pyramid—the center of the cyclone, so to speak. And then came the words: *mindset, motion,* and *mystical.* And then the realization that these are the three pillars of zero limits living. All of this in an instant, all of this in a flash—and all of this is what I want to share with you now. This book will explain that image.

But let me make this real for you right now. Try this:

Think of something you've wanted. It can be anything. Person, place, or thing. Experience. No matter. Whatever it is that you've been wanting to have, do, or be, the reason it's been out of your reach has been because of some invisible barriers. Call them what you will—beliefs, programming, paradigms—they are unconscious limitations. You don't even know they are there. They are outside conscious aware-ness. The foundation I offer, the three pillars, will erase those limitations.

The pillars—mindset, motion, and mystical—support the experience of living with zero limits. This revelation has never been shared before. Why? Because it did not exist before. Again, you can go to my work and find pieces of it. While there's a whole category in personal development that talks about action and discipline, that, too, is only a slice of it. And, of course, you can look at mystical traditions and find lots of people, including me, who have written books about spirituality. But they end up treating spirituality and mysticism as if they're separate things by themselves, when we're actually spiritual beings having a human experience.

We need to be able to use all three pillars at once. This new strategy is where it all comes together. This combination of essentials takes my thirty-five-plus years of knowledge and experience and unites them into a cohesive whole. Together, the three pillars of zero limits living form what I call a *practical spirituality,* one that you can apply to your life. I'm excited, I'm inspired, and I can't wait to share it with you.

We are going to take a journey together through these three pillars. It is going to challenge your beliefs. It is going to be enlightening. It is going to be transformative. And it is going to open up a world of possibilities for you to live with zero limits.

WHERE WE'RE GOING: ZERO LIMITS

Before we look at the three pillars, let's peek ahead at our destination. What does it mean to live with zero limits?

By using those two words as actual literal interpretations, I'm offering you a way to live life from a new understanding: that *the limits we believe in, the ones that stop us from having whatever we want, are actually mental constructs*. We've either created those limiting beliefs on our own, or we've agreed to them because we heard or saw other people demonstrate them. And we just nodded our head, usually unconsciously, and accepted them as limits.

But what we're talking about is living a life without *any* limits. Notice how you respond to reading that, because it's likely to show you where you already have limitations in your mind. Maybe you thought, "Everybody has limits," or "You can't just do whatever you want." Maybe you thought, "YES!" or "I want that, Dr. Joe—show me how!" Your response wasn't good or bad; it was just a sign pointing toward your limitations. For now, notice your thoughts as you read these words. Listen to that voice in your head. Is it agreeing? Is it arguing? That voice is not the limitless you. It's the voice of your limitations.

Let me explain.

BEWARE

Those very words—zero limits living—are probably going to bump up against your existing beliefs and paradigms: a mindset you already have, whether you're aware of it or not. Part of you is probably saying, "Well, zero limits sounds really exciting, but I know I'm not going to be able to [fill in the blank]." That feels true to you because that's where your mindset is. So, I'm teasing you just a little bit and planting, very delicately, a little seed that we'll explore in the first pillar. And that seed can grow and point the way to where we're going: the world of zero limits.

Consider: What would life be like for you if there were no limits? I'm not just talking about speed limits when you drive your car, but rather zero limits when you live your life. What would you welcome if you knew it was entirely possible?

WHAT STOPS US FROM TAKING THE JOURNEY TO ZERO LIMITS?

Your first decision is to go on the journey in the first place. What got you here isn't going to get you *there*. What's happened before probably isn't going to help you get to where you want to be. We're going to have to change a lot of limiting beliefs. We'll do it in bite-sized chunks, but you need to be open to looking at yourself and receiving new ways of being.

Pause here and listen to those little voices in the back of your mind when I tell you we're going on a journey to zero limits living. How are they already trying to stop you? What parts of you don't want to pack your bags and hit the road? What do you hear in your head?

And now, let's begin to change the old, limiting mindset.

First, we need to believe the journey is doable and the destination exists. Lots of people may pick up this book, page through it, and think, "This won't work for me. This isn't going to work for me because of my upbringing, because of my parents, because of my mental and emotional health, my education, my religion, the country I'm in . . ." You get the idea.

Any number of things that people may or may not be consciously aware of lead them to believe that *this very tool or therapy or modality works for everybody else.* Does that sound familiar? "It works for Dr. Joe, might work for a few other people, but it's not going to work for me."

That is a great example of a limiting belief. It's not the truth. It's not a fact. It's not scientifically proven that you are the one for whom this won't work. What it is, is a *belief*. And that's all part of *mindset*, which is the first pillar we're about to jump into.

So, what do you need to pack? Well, look at the image of my thunderbolt. The pyramid rests on a foundation (which I'll explain in full as we move along). You need a strong mental foundation to build your three pillars on, and that mindset foundation is made up of your beliefs, your desire, and your need for change. If you set those as your foundation and stay open to them, amazing things will happen.

But let me make this real for you. Think of something you would want if you allowed yourself to admit it. Be honest. More money? New car? New house? Relationship? Romance? Spirituality?

Nobody is looking. Go ahead and admit what you want. Write it down so it feels real. Look at it.

Now, notice your thoughts. *Are you doubting it is possible to have such a big dream?* Most likely you are. But why? Where are those doubts coming from? I'll tell you. They are in your mind as a preset series of beliefs. This is your current mindset. What you think is possible is based on your programming. But what if you erased your old programming and made zero limits living your new set of beliefs—your new mindset?

Of course, you still need to take action, which is why action (motion) is a separate pillar. And you still need the third, mystical pillar. Under both mindset and motion, there is an invisible field—an energy field that is actually alive. It's where you are getting energy and where you can go for answers. That's the mystical pillar.

I realize all of this needs explaining. So, let's hit the road together. Along the way, we're going to work with the three pillars: mindset, motion, and mystical. Their strength comes from how they all work together—mindset and mysticism inform motion, for instance—so this won't be a linear path; rather, it'll loop back on itself.

We'll start with exploring how our mindset can make or break our zero limits living.

We cannot solve our problems with the same thinking we used when we created them.

—ALBERT EINSTEIN

Pillar 1

MINDSET

Each pillar will have its own little "aha!" moment for you, but this one may have many. In the mindset pillar, we want to look at how you're thinking and how that limits your awakening. We want to look at what you currently believe. We want to look at your paradigms, your view of life. This exploration has three parts: your paradigm, intentions and counter-intentions, and brain hacks.

Your mindset is the compass that directs the course of your life. With a positive and determined mindset, you can navigate any challenge and unlock limitless potential. It's not about what happens to you, but how you choose to respond that defines your journey.

YOUR PARADIGM

A paradigm is how you believe the world works. It's your particular philosophy. You probably never thought that you have a particular philosophy (unless you've read philosophy

books), but you do; you live your life from a set of param-
eters that are largely invisible to you. It's a little bit like the
fish that's in the water but doesn't know what water actually
is. It just experiences water as, "This is life."

Earlier, I mentioned how I was homeless and in poverty for a big portion of my life. When I looked around, I
thought the world was out to get me. I thought it was set up
to be me against the planet, me against the universe. And
because of that mindset, I did not see opportunities. I did
not see optimism. I did not see choice. I did not see or experience happiness. I believed, like we all believe, that what I
perceived was the truth.

But what was the truth? The truth was that I was seeing
what I was seeing because of my belief system.

A mindset, or a paradigm, is how you view the world.
Now, here's where I go beyond anything I've ever taught
before. I've created courses on empowerment—I wrote
The Awakening Course, for example, and I created Miracles
Coaching®, my trademarked and proven system for change.

Now I want you to look so deeply at the idea of beliefs
and mindset that you realize how all of the beliefs or any
mindset you can name, whether victim or empowered, spiritually aware, transcendent—*any* kind of label you can put
on a mindset—is actually *still limiting your ability to live.*

Obviously, being empowered is better than being a victim, but what if empowerment is actually a limitation, too? What if there are more expanded ways of looking at life? If you've read my book *Zero Limits*; its follow-up, *At Zero*; or the follow-up to that, *The Fifth Phrase*, you know that there is a whole world of possibilities that is more available to us than we ever thought before—a whole lot that I didn't realize when I was homeless.

Here's an example of how being empowered can also limit you in living a life of zero limits.

About two thousand years ago, one of the great Stoic philosophers, Seneca, said, "It's all in your head. You have the power to make things seem hard, or easy, or even amusing. The choice is yours."

This is mind-blowing. This is Seneca, who was born in the year 4, pointing out that your mindset controls your personal experience. But I'm going to take you beyond where Seneca was, because even with his great insight, he had his own limits that he did not see.

I like the ancient Stoics and I've gotten much out of their teachings. They helped me through tough times when I went through a divorce and the pandemic. But I also think they're empowered victims—victims of their own mindsets.

I've read the key figures of Stoicism: Marcus Aurelius, Epictetus, and Seneca. The last is my man. Seneca's letters are as crisp and clear today as they were then. It's as though he wrote them to me personally. Yet, as much as I admire Seneca, I notice he has a "victim" or fatalistic attitude. Most of the Stoics did. They felt you could control yourself, but not anything external to you.

That sounds wise, right? But the Stoics didn't have access to modern science. The world of quantum reality is proving we can influence life just as life influences us. For the Stoics, the only thing they could influence was their own mind. Seneca wrote, "Everything hangs on one's thinking." He's right, but there's more. Everything hangs on your thinking, your feeling, your doing, and your connection to the Great Something—the term I use for the mysterious higher power others may call God, Divine, Cosmos, Universe.

As we look at mindset, which is how you view the world, can you begin to look at your own? The simplest aspect is, do you think the universe is a friendly place? Do you think the world is on your side? Do you think you are alone in the universe? Do you think it is a benevolent universe, actually out to help you survive and prosper?

Or do you think, like I did when I was homeless, that the universe doesn't care at all? I believed the universe would break my back and leave me on the side of the road.

How do you think about it?

EXERCISE: YOUR VIEW OF THE WORLD

When you think about the world—what you feel the world is, not what you want it to be—what's the first word that comes into your thoughts? Whether it's positive or negative doesn't matter; what matters is that it's the truth of what you believe.

If you begin to see that your paradigm is negative, take a breath. I can relate to struggling. I can relate to feeling like a victim. I lived in the Dallas Public Library in the late 1970s. I was in poverty for ten years. I can relate to the depression, the discouraging thoughts, and even the feeling that suicide is a way out.

I can relate to hopelessness. I want to make sure you understand that where you are in your life right now is only your current reality. It is not permanent. I want you to have hope so you begin to believe you can change. With the three pillars, you're going to get great information, but even more important than that, you will get the inspiration that melts the old mindset away and allows the light to shine through.

Layers of Belief Slow Spiritual Energy

We are spiritual beings having a human experience. We need to be able to have a great life—a luxurious life if we so choose—and to attract and achieve all the things we want to have, do, and be. This book is all about allowing that light to come through.

And what light am I talking about? The light of spirituality. When we get to the third pillar, the mystical, I will help you identify with that so you can allow it to come in. But for now, as I discuss the mindset pillar, I'd like you to imagine that there is the power of Spirit. And imagine that the power of Spirit is just unlimited energy (zero limits living again) available for you to create whatever you want. And it is trying to come through you right now.

What's stopping it are only layers of beliefs. Your mindset slows or blocks the spiritual energy that's trying to come in to create with you and for you. This is a big issue and a big statement, and obviously taking this on creates a new mindset for you. Instead of having a limiting mindset, you need a mindset empowered by Spirit itself.

As you're reading this, maybe you still have beliefs that say, "Well, this sounds great, but how's it going to work for me?" Or, "I'm stuck here and I can't get out of my job or out of my relationship or out of town." I want you to remember that this is only current reality. Current reality will change. It will change all by itself, because that's the nature of life. Life keeps evolving, keeps recycling things. It's always reforming energy and moving us around.

With the information in this book, you will learn how to create the new moments that you want. I want you to have an open mindset to hear me out and go through all three pillars so you can live this practical spirituality.

INTENTIONS AND COUNTER-INTENTIONS

If you know my work, or saw the movie *The Secret,* or you've read some of the success literature, you've heard of the law of attraction and the word *intention.* When you state what you want to have, do, or be, you're stating an intention. This is your desired outcome. This is your goal. The law of attraction teaches that because you're focused on this goal, you tend to pull it into your life. You tend to attract it.

The law of attraction is indeed a law. It's even a principle of psychology: William James, in his famous two-volume set, *Principles of Psychology,* from the 1800s, basically pointed out that you get what you focus on. That's the essence of an intention.

Some say the phrase *law of attraction* first appeared in print in 1877 in *The Secret Doctrine,* penned by Russian mystic Helena Blavatsky. Others say it was even earlier, in 1855, when it appeared in *The Great Harmonia,* written by the American spiritualist Andrew Jackson Davis. It was made popular in William Walker Atkinson's 1906 published book *Thought Vibration or the Law of Attraction in the Thought World.* In 1910, Wallace Wattles applied the law of attraction to wealth with his famous book *The Science of Getting Rich*. In the 1980s, Jerry and Esther Hicks, two clients of mine in the 1990s, started bringing the concept to the world with their messages attributed to Abraham. And, of course, the movie *The Secret* brought the concept to the screen beginning in 2006.

However, this book in your hands goes way beyond the law of attraction. Most people think the law of attraction means "what you think is what you get"—state an intention and you'll attract it. But that's incomplete and misleading. What I've discovered—and I think this has been my big contribution to the self-help movement, because I don't know anybody else who was talking about it when I was learning this—is the idea that *we have counter-intentions*.

What does that mean? I'll give you a great example. When I was homeless, I lived in the public library and read self-help books. I remember reading *Think and Grow Rich*, by Napoleon Hill, one of the greatest pieces of success literature of all time. I know millionaires who say they read it every year. I know people who say they've read it fifty times. I first read it while sitting on the library floor, by the bathroom where the water fountain was, and at the end of it, I looked around and said, "How come I'm not rich? How come I'm broke? How come I'm homeless?"

Remember, this is before the internet. We didn't have coaching. The only coaching back then was running Little League and football teams. I couldn't even have imagined such a thing as a self-development coach. Even if I could have, back in the late 1970s I couldn't have afforded one. I was trying to transform on my own. And, through a process of bloody knees and black eyes and going through the rough passages of life, I learned that, yes, intentions are powerful. State an intention for what you want to have, do, or be, *but then* listen to the voices in your head—your mindset—because more often than not, you'll hear a voice that, though it sounds very reasonable, will tell you why you can't have it.

That voice is your counter-intention. You will say something like, "I intend to attract more money. I want $5,000 of unexpected income," or, "a 50 percent increase in sales," or whatever it happens to be. But then, in your subconscious/unconscious mind, you have counter-intentions that say, "That'll never happen," or, "That can't happen in this economy." Or maybe you have beliefs just below your awareness that money is bad, money is evil, money corrupts. Then your unconscious might say, "If I'm successful, everybody will judge me. If I do really well, the tax man will come and take it all." We all have beliefs like that as part of our mindset. You can see how those beliefs run counter to your intentions and interfere with the law of attraction, right?

The idea of counter-intentions was a big discovery for me, which is why I started doing a lot of belief-clearing work. I wrote books and courses on that and created a mentoring program to help people with it. I created Miracles Coaching® to help people with this very issue.

What I invite you to do is listen to yourself. When you state an intention, immediately those voices go off, and you identify with them. You think those voices are you! One of the things you'll find out as part of your own awakening in this particular book, especially when we get to the mystical pillar, is that *you are not those voices*. Those voices are beliefs.

Very often, they're composites of voices you heard growing up, including your parents' voices, or your teachers', or your minister's. They told you how to get approval and love. You heard what they were saying, and you wanted their approval, and a part of your personality was created. And when you hear that voice in your head now, you don't realize that it came from those figures, but that's where you got the belief. It was never yours; you just adopted it.

There's an aspect of psychology called parts therapy that is designed to deal with these different voices, different parts of us. It doesn't mean we have schizophrenia or multiple personality disorder, but we do have aspects of us that, in a real way, are just trying to protect us. They don't want us to be hurt, and we listen to them . . . and end up living a very limited life. So when you state an intention and hear the voice that says, "Oh, that works for Dr. Joe. I've heard it worked for other people. Oh, I saw the movie where it worked for somebody, but it'll never work for me," that voice is a separate entity; it's not even real.

> *Doubts never end. If one doubt is removed, another*
> *takes its place. It is like removing the leaves of a tree*
> *one by one. Even if all the leaves are clipped off,*
> *new ones grow. The tree itself must be uprooted.*
>
> **—RAMANA MAHARSHI**

You Can Choose Your Mindset

What I'm inviting you to do in this first pillar is to realize that you can select your mindset. Too many people think, "Well, this is my personality. I can never change it. This is who I am." You hear that a lot: "This is who I am." But there's lots of recent research that disagrees. There's a riveting book called *Personality Isn't Permanent,* by Benjamin Hardy, PhD. He proves beyond a doubt that you can re-create your own personality. It is not set in stone. Part of the mindset we want to free ourselves from is believing that we're locked into certain ways of being.

Another thing I've often heard people say is, "Because of where I am, I can't escape it." They think that because they live in poverty, or the inner city, they can't change who they are or their circumstances. I remember hearing the actor Morgan Freeman say in an interview, "That's an excuse," and then describe the rough-and-tumble, poverty-stricken area where he grew up. "The bus leaves every day, man," he said, laughing. "The bus leaves every day." Every day you can escape your environment. I'm not saying it would be easy; just that it's possible. You can start over with where you live, with your personality, and with what you think.

You have intentions; now start paying attention to the counter-intentions. Hear those voices and don't automatically believe them. Question them! Is what they're saying true? Is it your belief, or someone else's?

When I was first learning to be a singer-songwriter, I attended a small class with Kevin Welch and Ray Wylie Hubbard, two well-known artists. Ray said he still had doubts whenever he performed or created. But he learned to ask an important question to remove those doubts: "Where's the proof?" Where's the proof he can't perform? Where's the proof he can't write a new song? As he discovered, there is no proof. None!

There's no evidence that you cannot re-create yourself, have an awakening, have the money you want, the life you want, the partner you want—whatever it happens to be. There is no evidence at all that you can't have it. What does that kind of statement do? It challenges your mindset. It helps you realize, "Well, if there's no evidence that I can't have it, maybe I can go for it. And maybe it'll come true."

Identifying Your Beliefs—and Your Counter-Intentions

I mentioned in the Introduction that a lot of what I'm saying is going to rattle your cage a little. It's going to bounce off of your existing beliefs. Just listening to your reactions as you read this book is one way to reveal those beliefs. If you say something equivalent to, "This won't work for me," then "This won't work for me" is your belief, your mindset, and in this case, your counter-intention.

Yet, consider: It is not your fact. It cannot be proven. There is no evidence that this won't work for you. It is simply your belief, and whatever belief you happen to have right now *is not reality*. You can make it reality by fueling it with your attention and then acting as if it's real—but until you do, it's not real.

Once, I was talking with a woman about affirmations, which are statements you say to yourself to reprogram your mindset, to think more positively. And she said, "I tried affirmations. They didn't work for me."

I thought for a minute and said, "Do you realize what you just said is an affirmation? You said, 'Affirmations don't work for me,' so you are affirming that affirmations don't work for you. And then when they *don't* work for you, you actually proved that affirmations *do* work for you."

Her eyes crossed but I think she understood.

We get into circular thinking that we mostly can't see in ourselves because we don't question it—which is why I think coaching and mentoring are so important. But you can get these "aha!"s from listening to yourself, and obviously from this book.

For now, pay attention to your thoughts. This is your mindset; this is you rewiring your own brain. It's your software, and you can change it. I'd like you to be aware of it so you can transcend it.

If you are making affirmations to attract love, money, or enlightenment, but underneath you don't actually believe it can happen, what's underneath it is the counter-intention.

When you say, "I want to attract something," but you are vetoing it with your counter-intention, what you need to look at is that opposing affirmation. Why do you believe it? Why do you think it's not possible? What's the evidence for you to actually support your failure rather than your success?

EXERCISE: FINDING YOUR COUNTER-INTENTIONS

- Write down something you want very much to have, do, or be.
- Listen for those voices in the back of your head. What do they say? What doubts or blocks come up to tell you that you can't have what you want?
- Now refute that voice. Say what you choose to believe instead.

For example, you say you want a new car. Okay. You deserve it. But then the voice in your head says, "No, you don't deserve it." Or, "How will you pay for it?" Or, "What will my family think?"

You now give the opposite argument to each statement: "I DO deserve it." "I'll pay for it one month at a time." "My family will be inspired by me."

Get the idea?

I want you to remember that everyone struggles. My love, Lisa Winston, played the movie *The Secret* the other night for whatever reason. She began fast-forwarding to find the parts where I was in it. We both had a nice chuckle every time the fifteen-years-younger version of me would show up on the screen and talk. In the movie, you get to hear different people's stories. John Assaraf tells about being in a street gang. Jack Canfield talks about being a broke schoolteacher making maybe $8,000 a year. I tell my story of being homeless, and then they make the point that everybody has a similar story.

We've all been through something. Usually not very pleasant; usually pretty rough. And we've come out the other side. If you are going through something right now, know that you're not alone, and you will come out the other side—and, in fact, you will thrive and prosper by being illuminated with what you're reading here.

BRAIN HACKS

We've looked at your paradigms and your counter-intentions, two important parts of the mindset pillar. Brain hacks are a third way we can change our mindset to help instead of hinder us.

Brain hacks are shortcuts to getting results by leveraging how your brain works. You can trick your brain into manifesting what you want in life. This works because the scientific evidence shows that your brain does not know the difference between reality and imagination.

When people first hear that, they say, "Oh, give me a break. My brain knows the difference between reality and imagination." Think about the last time you had a dream, whether it was really erotic or really scary, and when you woke up, your body was responding to that dream. But the dream wasn't real, was it? The dream was in your imagination. What if we use this little loophole of the brain to manifest what you want? The brain responds to imagery, emotion, and repetition. Let's look at how we can use each one to strengthen your intention.

Imagery

The first brain hack is to name an intention you'd like to have, do, or be. Now, find (or create) an image that represents what you want to manifest. This is why so many people create vision boards out of posterboard. They cut out pictures of what they want and paste them on the posterboard. Then they look at the posterboard as many times as they need to throughout the following days, weeks, months, years. What they're doing is programming their mind. They're saying, "This is what I want," knowing that the brain responds to the image. So, the first brain hack is to find or create an image that will provoke this response. There are apps to help you with this, such as Mind Movies.

Emotion

The second hack is to use emotion. It is another tried-and-true fact that three things can get our attention: what we love, what we hate, and what we fear. This explains why so many people on social media complain, mentally go to fear and hate, and find themselves with more fear and hate. They're attracting it. They're using their brain to shoot themselves in the foot.

The vast majority of people are unhappy. They don't realize they have a choice. But more importantly, they don't realize they are focusing on emotions that just bring about more experiences to feel more of the same emotions. This is basic law of attraction: you get what you feel.

What's a better approach? Look at the image of your intention with love, with gratitude, with passion, with longing. Strengthen your intention with positive emotion.

In other words, look at the image of what you want with a heart open to receiving it, not a mind complaining about how you won't receive it. Look with love. Look with curiosity. Look with a happy expectation of receiving it soon.

Repetition

The third brain hack is repetition. Just as the negative things you believed about yourself wired themselves into your brain the more you told yourself they were true, you can likewise create a positive groove in your brain for your intention.

Look at your image with as much love as you can, as many times as you can. Put that little image on your phone.

Set a timer to go off for any amount of time you like, say, once an hour, to remind you to look at the image. Repeat this as you go to sleep and when you wake up. These are all ways to leverage what neuroscience teaches us. This brain hack will help you accelerate the attraction of what you want.

Here's what happens when you program your brain this way. Consciously, you make an intention. Consciously, you find the image. Consciously, you look at it with love. Consciously, you repeat all of this. These actions help you move your intention into your subconscious mind. The repetition buries it in the subconscious. The subconscious is more active and more powerful and more connected than your conscious mind. The subconscious goes to work, without you knowing anything about it, to manifest what you want.

But here's what also takes place, which nobody's ever described in this way before. As you keep doing this, your intention goes beyond your unconscious into what Carl Jung called the *collective unconscious*. The collective unconscious to me is—and this is my own phrase for it—the *esoteric internet*. It is the wireless system that connects all of us.

The esoteric internet is where you and I and everyone are connected. Why is this important? As we drop our intention into it, the intention travels the esoteric internet looking for those who can help manifest it.

Here's an example. A few years ago, there was a young man in Thailand who got the intuitive hit to contact me and offer an enormous amount of money to fly to Thailand and speak on his stage for his very first event. Now that I've made that trip, I know just how far away this place is. It is not a drive to the corner. This is a couple of days of flying.

But he sent his request to me, and obviously we ended up meeting. I heard his story. I eventually wrote a book with him. His book is a breakthrough. It's called *Homeless to Billionaire*, and it's by Andres Pira. And how did all this connection come about? Yes, on the superficial level, his office sent my office an email, but what was before that and what was deeper than that?

Andres had a strong desire to meet me. He later claimed I was the reason he survived homelessness and went on to become a billionaire. His desire was emotion. He kept visualizing meeting me. He of course repeated this, constantly thinking about my coming to Thailand. He naturally followed the three steps of programming the mind—image, emotion, repetition. His request went even deeper.

It went to the esoteric internet. This is where magic and miracles happen. And this is a brain hack that goes beyond the brain. It's a mystic hack happening in the collective unconscious. You create it by going to Source rather than only using your mind. The more you see what you want, feel it with love, and repeat that process, the more you program your subconscious and the further the order/request floats down into the esoteric internet. This is where magic happens.

As a result of Andres's inner work, his request touched me, albeit unconsciously. When his offer to visit Thailand slid across my desk, I almost said no. I almost passed. But *something* about his offer nudged something within me, and I agreed. I'm declaring that his intense and persistent request went into the esoteric internet and touched me on that level. This is the level of the mystical, which we'll get to soon.

I get off-the-charts excited talking about this because the implications are staggering. We talk about zero limits living—yet how can there be any limits when we go to the deep, collective, unconscious, esoteric internet, where we're all connected? Anything's possible!

So that's the first pillar, mindset. As you examine your worldview and beliefs, identify and unplug your counter-intentions, and harness the power of your brain, you are on the road to living a life of zero limits. Now it's time to take action!

Success seems to be connected with action. Successful people keep moving. They make mistakes but don't quit.
—CONRAD HILTON

Pillar 2

MOTION

The second pillar is *motion*. There are three kinds of motion: inspired action, refined action, and continuous action. Now, most people bundle these all together and say, "Oh, action is action. Action is just one step in front of the other, left foot, right foot. You know how it works." That's what my father used to tell me. But looking at each kind separately accelerates our journey. I've talked about inspired action before, in other programs and books; the other two are new to me, and all are part of the enlightening image that came to me in that lightning bolt of a moment. Let's discuss them all.

It always seems impossible until it's done.
—NELSON MANDELA

INSPIRED ACTION

Inspired action comes from inside of you. It is inner sourced—usually because you have an "aha!" experience—some sort of inspiration or intuitive hit. It comes from your own love and passion, and is fueled by whatever mission you're connected to on the mystical level.

What's the difference between inspired action and just action?

Say you're working for some carpenter and they tell you, "Go cut up these 2×4s—and we need seventy of them." You're going to take action, but it's not necessarily inspired action. It is action for pay. You do it to get an end result, a paycheck. I worked on the railroad starting at five years old. My father was the supervisor and took me to work with him. And this was no picnic; he actually had me doing labor on the tracks. Later, he took me to work when he had construction jobs on the railroad. I worked every summer and weekends throughout my life. When I was a teenager, I lied about my age—with my father's encouragement—and I was hired by the railroad to work all summer. I did this until I was around twenty-five or thirty, so I know what that kind of action is. It's often just labor.

Inspired action is different. Inspired action is between you and the mystical—a word I use because that's the nature of this whole program. It's between you and the deeper aspect of spirituality. This goes past the level of the lumberyard and the 2×4s. We're going deep into the energy vortex of life. We're going to where things are created in the invisible fourth-dimensional realm, if you will, and show up in third-dimensional reality. A railroad track exists in third-dimensional reality, and so does a home being built, but the vision for it is actually in the fourth dimension. Inspired action comes from a deeper source. It's unique to you.

I've written lots of books, usually because of an inner prompt that ignites my interest. I think writing any book is usually inspired action. I receive an idea and I honor the idea by sitting down to start typing. In short, inspired action is inner sourced. Maybe your picking up this book was inspired action, too.

But what about when you get all fired up and inspired, yet never take the next step? When you say "no" to a road inviting you down itself?

This is a loss of such depth and degree that it can never be measured, because you did not take the action you knew you wanted to take and felt inspired to take. You are left with zero. And I don't mean a *zero limits* kind of zero. I mean zero in terms of the emptiness of nothing. There is no feedback. There's no result. There's no product; there's no service. There's nothing to brag about. No story to tell.

> *Don't wait. The time will never be just right.*
> —NAPOLEON HILL

The Cascading Results of Inspired Action

As I've mentioned, I've recorded many music albums. If they were only ideas, I would be sitting here saying, "Well, I wanted to be a musician at one point, but I never actually went into the studio. I never took any action." You would not be interested, and I probably wouldn't bring it up because there would not be any real story to tell, except maybe one of a lost prize.

And that's what is really missing. If we don't take action, we have lost the prize of the story—be it the prize of the chase, the prize of the result, the prize of profit, whatever. We also lose the prize of connections, because taking action leads to other results that we can't predict until we take the action in front of us.

What you don't see until you begin are all the wonderful synchronicities, rewards, acknowledgments, surprises, and unexpected joy that comes from taking that one inspired action.

For instance, I wanted to be an author when I was a teenager. I took inspired action and started writing books. Being a published author was my only goal, but as soon as I became a published author, I got invited to be in a movie, one that made history—*The Secret*. I never would have been invited had I not written a book (*The Attractor Factor*) that the producer picked up and thought was so good, she called me up and said, "I'd like you to be in my movie about the law of attraction."

I had that happen when I performed with my Band of Legends for the very first time. I was a nervous wreck, but I thought, "You know what? I'm inspired to do this. My band wants to do it." I went onstage with them, we delivered, and we got a standing ovation.

But there was a bonus I didn't see coming. There was a woman in the audience who walked up to me and said, "I'm a movie director and I'm filming a movie. I have a part I think you'd be great in. Have you ever done any acting?" I thought, "I haven't acted since I was in kindergarten, and that was being one of the Three Little Pigs." But out loud I said, "Yes," and I was in a movie called *Cecilia*. You can see its listing on the Internet Movie Database.

My whole point is when you take inspired action, not only do you get the benefit of that action and all the results and trophies and anything else that comes along with it, but *that action also leads to new actions*, which could be amazing. There are so many levels of rewards from taking inspired action that it's hard to name them all.

"Am I Going in the Right Direction?"

I often get asked, "How do you know if the inspired action you're taking is the right action? How do you know you're going in the right direction?"

The action you take is always in the right direction. Stop and think about the first pillar—mindset. If you think, "Oh my God, what if I take this action and it's the wrong action?" that's a counter-intention, right? A new mindset would be, "This action that I take, no matter what it is, is absolutely the best one and correct one."

Why is it the best one? Because it's the next action you are taking. I'm talking about *choosing a mindset that approves of it*.

It is a tremendous fallacy and a black hole to think that any action you take is a mistake. Actions you take lead in a new direction because they always bring feedback. They are never failure. They are always feedback. The feedback tells you, "Well, maybe I need to adjust what I just did and do something differently in the next action step. But the action step I just did was absolutely perfect." Why was it perfect? Because that was the action step you took. And then what did you get as a result of the action step? You got information. That information helps you tweak what you want to do next. It's all good.

REFINED ACTION

Let me tell you a quick story to show you what refined action is. I told you I had been in poverty. While there, I was still working on myself, going to the library, reading, trying to be a writer, and eventually writing books. I had written a little book called *Zen and the Art of Writing*. I couldn't find anybody to publish it. Remember, this was the early 1980s: no internet. But I was learning about direct mail and direct marketing, which back then included classified ads. I thought, "Well, what if I took my book apart and turned it into a correspondence course?"

That's what I did. What began as a book became a correspondence course. I scraped up enough money to run a classified ad in *Writer's Digest* magazine. I used the old two-step marketing approach, where you run the ad with a free offer and they have to write to you to redeem it. The second step is to send them more information, hoping they make a purchase.

I was beginning to sell the five-part course based on the five chapters in the original book. What looked like a failure became feedback, which prompted the thought, "Well, what I'm doing right now isn't working as a book, but let me try it as a correspondence course." I just used the feedback and adapted it. And after a little bit of that, I did find a publisher, I transformed the course back to book form, and I sold it. My first book, *Zen and the Art of Writing*, was published in 1984.

Were any of those steps that didn't work out the way I expected them to failures? No. They all became feedback that I used to redirect my aim. There are countless stories like this in businesses around the world, where something they were trying didn't work, but along the way they found something else that ended up being the big win. The first step wasn't ever a mistake.

HOW REFINED ACTION HELPS YOU NOT GIVE UP

Any course can be corrected. Any momentum can be redirected. But if you don't take that first step, there's no momentum. There's no progress. There's no experience. There's no learning, and you'll never get where you want to be. So, again, there's no such thing as imperfect action because momentum is progress.

If we give up when we don't see immediate results, none of the cascading results of inspired action can show up.

This is an example of how all the pillars work together. It's why some of the pillars that are taught separately, like mindset, don't complete the job for people, because the rest of the story has been left out. To use the second pillar, motion, we have to lean into and use the first one, mindset. When we have that urge to give up, where's that coming from? That's our mindset. We have to take charge of our mindset first.

I was deeply influenced by Jack London when I was growing up, and his autobiographical novel, *Martin Eden,* greatly inspired me. London wrote, "Don't loaf and invite inspiration; light out after it with a club."

This is a guy who got up every day and wrote a thousand words. Every day. He created a discipline for himself. Jim Rohn said, "You can have the discipline of success or the discipline of regret." So when you have the discipline of taking action, you start to feel successful and get results. Jack London wrote fifty-some books. He only lived to be forty years old, so he wrote these over a very short period, but he disciplined himself not to wait for inspiration, to actually get up every day and start writing. Rather than give up when he didn't get results, he took control of his mindset and continued on his path.

A funny side story: I have a friend from Australia who also loved Jack London. He came to America and visited Jack London Park in California, where he read an inscription about how London wrote one thousand words daily and felt inspired by it. But by the time he got back to Australia, he had misremembered it. He thought it said that Jack London wrote *two* thousand words every day. My friend began to write two thousand words every day. As a result, he's written eighty-seven books. When he finally found out he was off by a thousand words, he backed off—and he felt like he was on vacation.

It's all how you look at things. When I was broke and homeless, I said, "I want to be an author. I want to write books that make a difference. I don't know how, I don't know when, but I'm just going to get up every day and keep doing it." There were certainly days that I didn't want to do it or felt like giving up. I almost did give up a few times, but—and this is the secret to keeping that momentum going—I continually reminded myself of the inspired goal. What is the inspired mission? What is the reason I'm doing this? I changed my mindset from discouragement to determination.

Again, this is why this whole program is so important and so different from everything else. I've written books such as *The Awakened Millionaire* in an attempt to get people to blend the material with the spiritual. But what I'm talking about here is *actually living from the spiritual level* so it becomes practical spirituality. Because it's spiritual first, it's easier for you to be continuously inspired. You're not doing it for egoic reasons. You're doing it for spiritually inspired reasons. This is why the next pillar, mystical, is so important. For us to live a life of zero limits, we need all three pillars.

Refined action is how you look at or evaluate the actions you've taken. If you're looking at them as failures, or if you're embarrassed by them, then your mindset isn't allowing you to see the positive results of that action. When we come to refined action through the lens of spirituality, anything can happen.

CONTINUOUS ACTION

Motion takes three forms: inspired action, refined action, and continuous action. This last one is as important as the other two.

Recently, an interviewer asked me, "Out of everything you've read and everything you've taught and everything you've written, what's the one thing that always works?" What a great question. I ended up saying, "Action"— but not just any action. Continuous, nonstop, persistent, never-give-up action.

I love this quote from Calvin Coolidge (it was probably written by Bruce Barton, according to my research, but it's attributed to President Coolidge). He said, "Nothing in this world can take the place of persistence. Talent will not. Nothing is more common than unsuccessful men with talent. Genius will not. Unrewarded genius is almost a proverb. Education will not. The world is full of educated derelicts. Persistence and determination alone are omnipotent."

I would say that's why "action" appears three times on the image of my thunderbolt of inspiration.

When I published my first book in 1984, I didn't know that there'd be another eighty books. But when I got an idea, I wrote another book. When I got yet another idea, I wrote another book. It was continuous action, which creates a momentum that wedges itself in the universe. This goes back to the esoteric internet or the collective unconscious. The more you take continuous action, the more you send your energy into the collective unconscious. And at some point, the whole world awakens to who you are.

This is why a lot of people who have been working for decades suddenly get noticed overnight. Everybody says, "Wow, that singer came out of nowhere. That actor just burst upon the screen." But if you read their biographies, you find out, no, they've been consistently working for *decades*, mindfully holding their desire for success. That continuous action kept sending their signal into the esoteric internet. They're obviously winning along the way because they're doing what they love—they're taking inspired action.

Let's take a closer look at this step.

When you state your desire/intention/goal, you set up a target. Your mind knows where you want to go. As you bring the goal to life with an image, positive emotion, and repetition, you drive the desire into the esoteric internet.

Your seed is now planted. As a result, you will begin to get ideas, nudges, gut feelings, intuitive hits, and more on action steps you can take. It's important to take them, even when there is no evidence they will lead anywhere. You have to trust. Have faith. Act. And, as you act, you will start a ripple in the universe.

> *There are no limitations to the mind*
> *except those we acknowledge.*
> **—NAPOLEON HILL**

GETTING STARTED ON ANY ACTION

People have a few common difficulties with taking that first step of inspired action: being overwhelmed by their idea, not knowing where to start, and wanting to know how it's all going to work. Here, I discuss all three and offer hacks to defeat them.

Dealing with Overwhelm

A lot of people who don't take action often say they feel overwhelmed by their project. Yet, how do you eat an elephant? One bite at a time. Okay, I wouldn't eat an elephant either, but you get the idea. Break up the huge into small, doable chunks. The brain hack for overwhelm is to break the work up into smaller actions.

As an example, in the late 1990s, I wrote a book on P. T. Barnum, *There's a Customer Born Every Minute*. At the start of my project, I found his life overwhelming. He was the guy behind the circus as we know it, but also, over his eighty years, so much more—an entrepreneur, publicist, speaker, politician, marketer, author . . . it just went on and on. There was so much information that the only way I could manage it was to make a folder for every aspect of his life as I did the research. Then, when it came time to write, I just picked up a folder and wrote that chapter based on my notes therein. I ended up writing a book that has been well received and reprinted a few times. When you look at it, you'll get a sense of, "Oh, Dr. Joe had to do a lot of research to put this together." And I did! I just had to break it down into bite-sized steps.

Not Knowing Where to Begin

Another difficulty with starting something that people often use as an excuse is that they don't know where to begin. My rule of thumb is to begin right where your feet are. President Teddy Roosevelt said, "Do what you can, with what you have, right where you are."

Just use what's in front of you. If that's a sheet of paper and a pen, that's where you begin. There is always a tiny step that is easy to take. It could be to go get the URL for the website that you want to put up, or launch the DBA so you can cash checks when they start coming to you. Do little things, whatever they happen to be.

Wanting to Know the "How"

The third thing that stops a lot of people from taking action is that they want the whole map. They want to know how things will work from here to the end.

There is no map. It doesn't exist yet. It will only exist after you've created it. Steve Jobs said, "You cannot connect the dots looking forward. You can only connect the dots looking backwards." What that means is, as you look forward to whatever it is—writing your book, opening your business, meeting the love of your life—you don't know all the steps that are going to manifest that for you. You only know the first step. But as you take that first step, the second one becomes apparent. You take that one. By the time you get to the end, you can look back and see the whole road that got you there, but the road was paved by you. At that point, when you accomplish your goal from all these actions you've taken, you can turn around and explain the story. You can say, "Oh, that dot led to that dot, which led to this dot." But at the beginning, those dots aren't lit up because they don't exist.

EXERCISE: GETTING STARTED

Write down what you want. Then sit quietly and see what occurs to you as a possible next step. Or write down a series of first steps. Then, as soon as you can, act on the steps you can accomplish. Note how you feel. Note what happens next. Don't be quick to judge or dismiss anything. As I quoted Bruce Barton in my book *The Seven Lost Secrets of Success*, "One never knows when he enters an elevator or opens an envelope, what turn of fortune awaits."

WHAT IS SUCCESS?

Once you've taken inspired, refined, and continuous action, it's important to look at how you measure the results. Most people have a type A mindset that would say, "Well, the results that count are making money, or somebody giving me an endorsement, or me bartering for something." They're looking for the concrete exchange. And what I'm pointing out in the three pillars of zero limits living is *we're going for an energy exchange.*

What counts about your actions is, are they coming from your spiritual inspiration? Writing books is fun and inspiring for me. It may be unpleasant for you. I'm not interested in paint pouring, but it brings my love, Lisa, alive. Each person is propelled by something different that is part of their spiritual mission.

The question to ask is, "What makes me come alive?" What actions feel good to you? When you take the action, acknowledge that it is successful not because of some practical result, but because it generated what you really wanted: the energy exchange. Simply taking action is moving forward to your goal of zero limits living.

> *Don't ask what the world needs. Ask what makes you come alive, and* go do it. *Because what the world needs is people who have come alive.*
>
> **—HOWARD THURMAN**

Pillar 3

MYSTICISM

The third pillar is what enlivens your action—and what makes a zero limits living mindset possible. It's dealing with the field of all possibilities, the energy source of all life, the Infinite Intelligence that can guide us all. At the mystical level, there are no limits. None.

Let's go back and combine this spiritual pillar with the pillar of mindset. The spiritual mindset is not one where we are reaching and grabbing for goodies all the time. This mindset realizes you *already have* all the goodies you can want. Now let me explain this, because it's a cornerstone to a lot of what I teach today, and it's very important to the three pillars program.

Believing in the power of the unseen is like having a secret weapon that fuels your dreams and propels you toward success. When you have faith in something greater than yourself, the universe conspires in your favor, and the path toward your goals becomes clearer and easier. Trust in the unseen and you'll achieve results beyond what you ever thought possible.

BEING IN THE NOW

There are at least two ways to look at miracles. The way most people see them is that something unexpected happens, and they say, "Oh, it was a miracle. I didn't see that coming. I didn't expect that. Oh my God, look, that's a miracle." I accept that. But the other kind of miracle—the one Einstein endorsed and Helen Keller talked about—is the *miracle of now*.

That's the whole message of a book I wrote called *The Miracle*. All of the longing for something else is taking us away from the reality and the power of this particular moment. The past is gone. It's only a memory, wispy and inaccurate. Studies show that we don't remember things accurately at all. We get upset and drive ourselves crazy over pictures in our minds that are inaccurate, often totally erroneous, and don't exist any longer anyway—the events are over.

The past is gone. The future isn't here. And depending on what you believe in terms of science and quantum mechanics, the future may exist in a parallel universe. But for you in this form, in this particular reality, that future isn't here yet. You're going to create it out of this moment. *The present, this moment, ends up being the most important and useful point of power.*

The more we can be in this moment, the more we feel satisfied. That's the key. It doesn't mean we don't still want a new car or a new house or more wealth or whatever it happens to be. But it will mean that, in this moment, we're satisfied.

I used to quote a woman I met in Hawaii almost thirty years ago. She had this statement at the bottom of all of her emails—she might still do so. It read, "I'm totally satisfied. I just want more." I loved it.

Can you imagine being totally satisfied and complete while acknowledging a desire for more? Because this mystical third pillar tells us that everything is abundant. There is no shortage. If somebody is sitting there thinking, "There's only one piece of pie and I'd better grab it," then they're probably going to grab it. But if they're thinking, "There's lots of pies, not just the one sitting right here. If I just hang out a little bit, the world of pies will open up for me, and I can have an abundance of them," *that* is a spiritual mindset.

Said another way, being open to something better than anything you can name opens you to guidance from the spiritual side of life. I've been teaching since around 1995 that whenever you state an intention, always end it with the phrase, "This or something better." The phrase becomes a way to open your mind to receive from the divine. Your mind doesn't know what is possible in the universe, but the divine does. Using this disclaimer phrase allows the third pillar to work for you.

THE I OF YOU

On my image, you can see three things combine to be the pillar of mysticism: the "I of you," asking and receiving, and awakening.

When I received the thunderbolt inspiration, the "*You*" was what came first. I didn't know the reason why at the time, but now I do. *You* was there first because it doesn't refer to your personality; it's referring to the divine you.

Before you got your name, you were the unknown. Inside of your body, inside of your flesh and bones, was an essence. Some people call it a spiritual essence. Some people call it the soul. Others have different names for it, given their religion and culture. Depending on the mindset we grew up with, we use various words when we attempt to describe what this invisible inside energy is.

I'm using *the I of you* to mean the divine I. Let me go one more step to explain this.

I first wrote about Ho'oponopono, a Hawaiian healing modality, in *Zero Limits*. I was deeply influenced by the therapist who taught it to me, Dr. Hew Len. Dr. Hew Len was a therapist at a mental hospital for the criminally insane, where he helped heal almost all of its inmates. These people were shackled and regularly sedated because they were dangerous, but the doctor helped heal them by using Ho'oponopono.

What was he doing? He was working on *his own inner perceptions* of the inmates. As he looked at them and felt repulsed or angry or afraid or whatever it was, he used the basic four phrases of Ho'oponopono: "I love you," "I'm sorry," "Please forgive me," and "Thank you." He said those phrases inside himself, as a type of prayer or petition to what he called the divine. He was working to bring himself to unconditional peace. The more he could find peace in the midst of chaos, the more the outer world changed and reflected his inner peace. The inmates responded by getting healthier.

Ho'oponopono is a tool you can use to benefit your mindset. It's an action you can take. But here's what's important for the third pillar. When Dr. Hew Len and I worked on the first book about this philosophy, *Zero Limits*, he would send me emails when we weren't meeting in person that would always end with "Peace of I." That's the divine. He wanted me, and he wanted for everybody, to have the inner peace that the divine has.

The *I of you* is the divine within you. Inside yourself, under your self-conceptions, beyond your emotions and thoughts and feelings, is this witness, this source, this energy field that we can call I. When you identify with the I of divinity rather than the I of your personality, you move to the unlimited power source.

When you identify with yourself and your personality, your mindset limits you. It limits what you think is possible because that is how you were trained. It's how your personality was programmed, so to speak. When you go past it to the I of divinity that's within you, that I doesn't have any limits. It cannot possibly have any limits. By its very nature, it's unlimited, so *the I of you lives within zero limits.*

Here's where your mindset is crucial. If you are not open to the idea of finding that inner witness, the inner Source, the I of you, then your mindset alone will prevent it from happening. This is why the first pillar helps us understand that our mindset—our personality—is software. We've been wired in a particular way, but we're not the wiring. We're not the software, and we can rewire, re-create, redo, and remake it in whatever way we would like. Mindset can enable us to find divinity within us or actually block it through our own blindness to it.

We really need to look at what we believe.

As I was writing this book, I was intuitively led to a new book called *The Awakened Brain,* by Lisa Miller. It reveals the scientific discovery that not only is the spiritual real but also that a part of our brain corresponds to it. This region "awakens" when you consider a higher power or a connection to a more divine source. Science proves that mysticism is both real and necessary for you to have a balanced life.

This is exciting. Science proves zero limits living is real!

We ask ourselves, who am I to be brilliant, gorgeous, talented, fabulous? Actually, who are you not to be? You are a child of God. Your playing small does not serve the world.
—MARIANNE WILLIAMSON

Meditation

Meditation has long been seen as a tool to work with your mindset and dwell in the I of you. We've all been disconnected from Source to some extent. How do we change our mindset and reconnect fully? I'm going to lead you through a short meditation to bring you to Source. But first let's define meditation.

My favorite quote about meditation was on the very first T-shirt I bought on the internet, way back in the 1990s. It said, "Meditation is not what you think." In other words, if you're sitting there thinking, you're not meditating. You're contemplating. You're brainstorming. Your neurons are firing off, and you're paying attention to the chatter. Nothing wrong with contemplation. I like to contemplate, too, but I recognize it's not meditation.

"Meditation is not what you think" suggests that meditation is *behind* your thinking. This is the kind of meditation that I endorse. It's the kind where you pay attention to the background behind the thoughts. That background canvas is the level of mysticism.

The example I've heard from Buddhists is that meditation is like watching the sky as the clouds go by. You're not focusing on the clouds; you're focusing on the sky. In meditation, you're not focusing on the thoughts. You're focusing on the space behind the thoughts, almost as if the thoughts are appearing on a blackboard or a whiteboard. What you think comes from your personality, bubbling up automatically and organically from your brain. It will always come and go, arrive and pass. Meditation can help you connect to Source and to the witness inside, which takes you past your thoughts to the space between and behind them.

The Whiteboard

Imagine a blank whiteboard. We can think of it as the universe. And like the universe, it has zero limits. Nothing is there. It is the field of all possibilities. You can request anything you want, and you can receive anything you can imagine.

I once began a presentation—it's on YouTube at https://youtu.be/ZTViougNWKo—where I talk about Ho'oponopono by standing at a whiteboard. I asked the audience to talk about all the different ways people can change. As we kept coming up with answers, I wrote each one on the whiteboard.

As I kept recording them, guess what happened? The whiteboard disappeared. It was covered in black chalk. I explained to them how all that black chalk keeps us away from divinity. The whiteboard is divinity. The whiteboard is potential. The whiteboard is zero limits living. Anything we put on it—even positive stuff—can create a barrier between us and the whiteboard. You can go to the whiteboard and request anything you like. You can go to the whiteboard and receive inspiration from it. But you can only go to the whiteboard when you start removing the mindset, the interference, the thoughts between your essence and the whiteboard. Meditation helps you do that.

ASKING AND RECEIVING

The ability to ask and receive is the second aspect of the mystical pillar. We can't connect to the divine if our mindset is telling us it's not okay to want things, ask for them, and accept them.

How comfortable are you with asking for what you want or need and allowing yourself to receive it?

Asking and receiving is a choice. It comes from your mindset. Someone whose past programming tells them asking isn't a safe or acceptable thing to do is not going to ask. Another person with different programming from a different past may think, "It's totally fine to ask. I do it all the time."

Look at your own programming here. Is it serving you or not serving you? If you're afraid to ask, it sounds to me like it's not serving you, that it's prohibiting you from the goodness of life, which is your birthright. The only reason you don't have that goodness is because your mindset says, "Nope, not okay."

Change your mindset so you can say yes. Here's a little brain hack for that.

Decades ago, when I lived in Houston, I spoke onstage after José Silva, who was the founder of Silva Mind Control.

José used to say, "Any intention you have, any goal you have, should benefit you and at least three other people." I always loved it because it made a win, win, win for more than just you. It also took asking out of your own ego. By changing the feeling from, "Well, I'm only doing this for myself," which is very selfish, to, "Well, I would like to really have this experience, but I would like other people to benefit from it as well," you've just enlarged the benefit of receiving.

But keep in mind that we're only playing with mindset here. When we're at zero limits living and we're coming from the mystical, we don't have those kinds of opinions. There are zero limits there. The opinions about what's available, what can't be done, what you deserve, how big of a car, how big of an income—all of that comes from your limited thinking mindset.

The more we look at mindset, the more we take action in the direction of where we want to go, the more we connect to the mystical I of you, and the more we allow ourselves to ask and receive, the more we are able to create, manifest, attract, and share with the world.

At this level, truly anything is possible.

AWAKENING

That all sounds great. But I can hear you thinking, "How? How can I open myself up to living in divinity, living with zero limits?"

Here's how it's going to happen. I have created an experiential, guided awakening. I will take you to the door of awakening so you can step through it and experience Source, the divinity, the I of you. You can come back to this meditation regularly and allow it to gradually change your mindset and reconnect you with Source.

WITNESS
MEDITATION

Tip: Record this meditation guidance in your own voice, speaking slowly and softly, and then listen to the audio as many times a week as you like.

To begin, just take in a nice, deep breath, and let it out nice and slow and easy. Again, take in a nice, deep breath and let it out nice and slow and easy. You might notice your body relaxing even more as you breathe. Take in one more nice, deep breath, and let it out nice and slow and easy. It's good to relax. And as you're naturally relaxing, your eyes can close as you tune within while listening to the meditation.

And as you're listening, you have thoughts—maybe thoughts about what you're experiencing right now. Thoughts about what you've been reading. Thoughts are very natural and very organic. They just happen.

But notice you are not those thoughts. You can report on them. You can describe them. You can write them down, but you are separate from those thoughts. Instead, you are a witness to those thoughts.

And now notice your emotions, your feelings. Maybe you are elated, happy, tired, confused, curious; whatever you're feeling is totally fine. But like your thoughts, notice you're not your feelings. You can describe feelings. You can report on your feelings. You can write about your feelings, but you're separate from them, too. You're a witness to your feelings.

And now notice your body, whether you're sitting or lying down. Just notice how you feel in your body. Maybe you need to move a little bit, stretch a tiny bit, adjust your position. And as you're paying attention to your body, notice you're not your body. You can describe it, you can feel it, you can photograph it, you can write about it. You seem to be *in* your body, wearing your body, being a witness to your body.

And now, as you breathe and relax, review. You are not your thoughts. You have thoughts, but you're behind them, watching them. And you are not your feelings. You have feelings, but you are behind the feelings, witnessing. And notice you have a body, but you can be a witness to your body—you can watch your body.

So if you are not your thoughts and not your emotions and not your body, what are you?

You are the essence, the I, the witness, the observer behind all of it. That observer is Source. The background to your thoughts, your feelings, your body, is the alertness of the divine. And that witness is the same in me, your neighbors, your family, and everybody on the planet, though they may not know it. That I in you has zero limits. There are no boundaries. There are no limits. There are no walls. There is nothing between what you can create and what you can receive as inspiration. That witness is truly the unlimited you.

You can go to this inner Source any time by taking a deep breath, relaxing, closing your eyes, and bringing your attention inside—past your thoughts, past your feelings, past your body. And there, at Source, you can make a request for something you would like to have, do, or be, or you can receive inspiration for something you can do for the benefit of yourself and others. Throughout your day, pause, take a breath, and, as you relax, you can go inside. Take a good look at this background you: the I of you, the home of zero limits. You can make your life a walking meditation to constantly reconnect to the witness.

And now you can bring your attention back to the room you're in, to the present reality, to this moment. You can open your eyes and you will carry with you this connection to the I of you, the witness inside of you, that we're calling zero limits living.

Q & A

The following questions were submitted by people who attended the online course out of which this book grew, which was presented originally live. You can see the course description at https://www.drjoevitale zerolimits.com/3pillars-cb. Enjoy these select questions and my answers to them.

HAPPINESS AS A LIMITING BELIEF

A person who attended the online training that became this book asked, "If happiness is my greatest strength"—which is great; that's what we call a high-grade problem—"but it's also my greatest weakness, would that also be a limiting belief?"

Yes, it is a limiting belief, and I'll say why. The psychological research shows that, first of all, happiness is what drives us. Everything we do is an attempt to be happy. We can deceive ourselves because we think, "When I get the car, I'll be happy." And you will be happy for a moment. Then you'll look around and say, "Okay, when's the *next* car coming down the pike?"

We get deceived thinking that we're still looking for what will make us happy, when the miracle is now and happiness is now. The research also says that happy people tend to get what they want faster. Even as they're waiting to get what they want, they've obviously already got what they really wanted, which was happiness. They're already there.

The part of the question that bothers me a little bit is the part about thinking it's a weakness, because thinking it's a weakness is a judgment. Where's the judgment coming from? From mindset.

As I said at the beginning, a lot of this material is going to bump up against your mindset—your current beliefs. This is an opportunity for you to look at your beliefs.

When somebody says, "Happiness is my greatest weakness," that is a belief. That is not true for me. It is not true for everybody. It is not a scientifically proven element in the universe. This is your judgment, and your judgment is not serving you. I invite people to pay attention to what they're thinking and what they're saying; question it. If it's not serving them, they absolutely should change it. Part of the message of the first pillar is that the mindset is wiring, beliefs, and narration that you can change with intent and effort.

HOW DESIRES LIMIT US

"I'm trying to reconcile and heal my relationship and manifest him back into my life. How can we use Ho'oponopono in the right way to heal our relationships and reconcile with our loved ones?"

One of the most frequent questions I get is, how do I attract my spouse back? Or, how do I get my next-door neighbor or the woman at work or the man at work to become my mate? And to me, it is a severe limitation to think like that. Thinking there's only one person for you, or it has to be the person you found, is setting up a limitation. You're setting up a boundary. You're also setting up a disappointment.

Also, with nearly eight billion people on the planet, there is bound to be a match or two for you that may not be your ex or the person next door or the person at work that you've become focused on. Again, we want to dilute the beliefs and the neediness and the attachment, because at zero limits, there are no boundaries. At that place of the I of you, you don't have those kinds of attachments or needs. You've dropped them, and you're now more open to something better coming to you.

Ho'oponopono is all about healing *yourself*. Not anybody else, because in Ho'oponopono, all of what you think needs to be corrected are your perceptions about what you think needs correcting. It's all internal. Any way you look at it, this is back to the mindset, and finding the mindset that is actually spiritually empowering to you.

LETTING GO OF THE LIMITS THAT MAKE PEOPLE FEARFUL OF THEIR OWN SUCCESS AND PROGRESS

"In 2020, I recorded a phenomenal year with huge results, more than I expected, thanks to mindset. In 2021, since January, I

saw a negative trend, and now I'm around 60 percent less compared to last year."

The first thing to consider is self-awareness. The person asking this question is partially self-aware of what's going on. But the greater thing that would make the difference is the mastermind, the mentoring, the group experience. See, we don't usually see our own stuff because we are living from it. The mindset is how you look at the world, but you don't typically notice how you look at the world because you are automatically living out of that mindset.

This is why it's so important to have a coach or a mentor, somebody on the outside who can neutrally reflect back to you what you're thinking and doing, so you can look at it clearly and maybe see it for the very first time. And at that point, you can choose to change it. There are two paths to awareness. One is self-awareness, where you're doing it on your own. The other is hiring a coach, a mentor, and with their help really going into the deep dive and unearthing the limitations and the beliefs so that you can be free of them once and for all.

CLEARING A MINDSET ABOUT DEBT

"What would be an effective strategy to use for clearing and being free of debt? Should one focus on the actual debt or focus on wealth, and for how often?"

I never used to like debt, either, especially when I was broke, until I realized debt was actually potentially good. A lot of very wealthy people are tremendously in debt, and debt has helped them. Decades ago, I thought it would be a really wise thing to pay off all my bills. I did. I was debt free. But then later when I went to buy something that required credit, I had no credit. I had no credit because I had had no debt. I realized, "Wait a minute, debt is actually good." I'm not talking about being in overwhelming, crushing, "you're going to go bankrupt" kind of debt. But consider that some debt can be a positive.

Psychologically, we want to look at debt in a more positive way, because if we look at it from a negative standpoint, we draw our attention to it with more negativity. If you tend to attract into your life what you're fearing or what you're hating, if you're fearing and hating debt, you're going to bring more of it into your life. I say, reframe it and look at debt as a positive. It's a useful thing on your path to wealth.

I'd definitely be focusing on wealth. I'd be focusing on the healthy circulation of money, meaning money comes in and money goes out. Some of it will go to take care of your debt, and as you do that, more money comes in. A healthy circulation of wealth is where I think you really want to be. But again, look at your mindset and look at how you're speaking and acting. You might also read my book *Attract Money Now*, which is free at www.AttractMoneyNow.com.

HOW STORIES LIMIT YOUR EXPRESSION OF YOUR DIVINITY

"How do stories limit us?"

I said in the movie *The Secret* that everybody has a story. Somebody is in a gang, somebody is homeless. Somebody's a schoolteacher. We all have a story.

Everybody needs to look at their life experience as a story that can liberate or limit them. The person who is talking about what they went through with the trauma and so forth, they're focusing on the story as they remember it.

When we were talking about mindset earlier, I said there's a great book called *Personality Isn't Permanent,* by the psychologist Ben Hardy. I also talked about the idea that our memory is totally inaccurate. In fact, studies by Dr. Hardy show that every time we play a memory in our brain, we lose 50 percent of its accuracy. It keeps fading as we keep remembering it.

We're spending a whole lot of time making ourselves feel depressed, rehearsing ways of being that aren't encouraging or liberating us, because of an inaccurate memory of the story of how we were brought up. Now, believe me, this is my tough-love approach. I certainly can understand and feel and have empathy for the person asking the question or anybody going through anything. But this is about awakening. This is about going beyond the stories.

This is about changing your mindset to one that's spiritually enlightened. This is about taking the inspired action that comes from Source. This is about living from the mystical side. You are a spiritual being having a human experience. To the best of your ability, do your best to drop the baggage. There's nothing wrong with getting help if you need it. I have certainly done it through a divorce, pandemic, everything else. When I need help, I raise my hand and get it. That's also why I endorse having a mentor, having a coach, being in a mastermind group: so it's not just you trying to wrestle with demons. It's everybody helping you realize the demons vanish when you go to Source.

HOW TO CLEAR BAGGAGE

"I'm working on clearing my negative beliefs at work using Ho'oponopono. I can witness my beliefs, but sometimes when I have a stressful day, I feel like I have so much to clear. I would appreciate any advice on how to clear when feeling overwhelmed."

There are probably a thousand different physical techniques that you can do—taking a nap, getting a massage, having a warm bath, going for a swim, playing basketball, dancing, singing, even having a glass of wine. But I keep bringing it back to mindset because I want to be of the most service to everybody. And if somebody is overwhelmed, what you clear on, to use Ho'oponopono terms, is the feeling of overwhelm.

Why is somebody overwhelmed? Because of mindset. For a second, let's revisit Seneca, who said, "It's all in your head. You have the power to make things seem hard or easy, or even amusing. The choice is yours." I love that quote because he used the word *seem*. He was not denying that there was something going on in your life and that your tendency was to say, "Well, this is overwhelming." But Seneca was saying, well, you could make it seem hard, which would make it overwhelming. Or you could make it seem easy.

Or—and this is the big stretch—you could even make it seem amusing. Somebody has described the feeling of overwhelm; there are many ways to understand this—for example, maybe they have too much to do, too much work, too much homework, whatever it is for whoever it is. But Seneca reminds us that we have a choice in how we look at it.

How could some things be seen as amusing that are very tragic? We all face moments like this in life; the death of a loved one, whether a family member or friend or pet. Seneca suggests there is a way to see it differently. When somebody dies, I can look at that as hard or easy or as amusing. But how do I look at it as amusing? Somebody died!

Famed comedian Jerry Seinfeld lives for the joke—even in real life, off camera, he's reaching for humor. In fact, he's often said, "If you're not telling a joke or reaching for a joke, why are you talking?" He doesn't want to hear from you. Somebody on one of Jerry's shows said a friend of his died, and Jerry said, "Eh, enough of him anyway." He turned it into a joke. Another time a friend of Jerry's said, "Whenever there is a tragedy in the world, the comics have the jokes that night, but they don't say them because the world isn't ready to hear them yet." The point is, humor is there as an option. A choice.

The reminder is, we are here for an awakening. Somebody who says "I'm overwhelmed" has judged it to be that way. Thousands of years ago, Seneca was saying, well, you can judge it as hard. You can judge it as easy. You can also judge it as amusing. And when you choose easy or amusing, suddenly you're not overwhelmed anymore. Your entire life experience changed because you altered your perception.

PEOPLE BEING AFRAID OF YOUR POWER

"There seem to be a lot of people around me, neighbors and family, afraid of my power. I wonder how to stay in it. What can we do when family are your least supportive people?"

Napoleon Hill, who researched twenty thousand successful people over a twenty-some-year period, said, "One of the number one reasons people end up failing or not going for their dreams is that they listen to family and friends." One of my secrets to success, and the first thing I'd advise, is not sharing my dreams with just anybody. You would think at my level and my age, I would just go ahead and say, "Hey, here's what I'm going to do," and just tell anybody that will listen. I do not.

Why? I protect my dreams. I only share my dreams with somebody who can help me fulfill them. Someone who's going to listen, give me input, and not dismiss the idea. Who won't rain on my parade. But I would not go with one of my ideas to a family member, because I have learned through experience that they don't think like I do; they aren't open-minded. They're in a mindset of lack and limitation. And so I'm just not going to share it. I'll talk about the weather with those people—not my dreams.

The second thing I advise is having a support group. I'm a big believer in mastermind groups. I've had great success from various ones I've been involved with. Get in a mastermind group because like-minded support will be your safe place, where you can share your dream and get support for it. (I discuss mastermind groups further in the "Use the Third Mind" section later.) But when it comes to family and friends, talk about whatever they want to talk about. Keep your dreams protected and close to your heart.

CAN I USE THIS TO WIN THE LOTTERY?

"Can I win the lottery?"

I've had people on planes ask me about that when they find out about what I write or they recognize me from a movie or television show. I've had people send me emails about this, too. The short answer is, yes, you can use this to win the lottery. There are people who have already done it. There are YouTube videos. I remember one in particular where a woman saw *The Secret* and visualized winning the lottery. She took action. She bought the ticket and she won. I don't remember if it was $40,000 or $1 million, but it was substantial. She made a video and gave credit to the law of attraction and to the movie *The Secret* and different teachers in it.

So the first answer is *yes*. It will depend on your belief. Because as soon as I say *yes*, a lot of people say, "Oh, come on. I can't *really* win the lottery." They are already eliminating the possibility with their mindset. Then the deeper level is, why do you want to win the lottery? Most of the time, they're afraid. They're afraid they're going to be in crushing, everlasting debt. They're afraid of lack and limitation. They're afraid of continuous struggle. This is why understanding your mindset is so important. Think back to when we talked about the brain hacks and how the brain responds to the energy of emotion: if you're afraid, you're focusing on the very thing you don't want—lack.

In that mindset, you're not going to win the lottery. Focusing on winning the lottery when you are afraid of money, when you probably even think money corrupts or money is evil, or there's not enough to go around, and you cannot get money in any other way, shape, or form—then the only thing you're betting on is a lottery ticket. All of that is a recipe for failure in terms of getting what you want.

All of this is about awakening. Wanting to win the lottery and not understanding why you want it comes from a mindset of limitation. It's not coming from a mindset of zero limits living.

Most people reading this have at one time or another thought, "Oh, can I win the lottery by using this material on zero limits, or Ho'oponopono, or the law of attraction, or [fill in the blank with any other tool or technique]?" But you have to go deeper to understand why you want it.

I went to Kuwait once. The woman who brought me there was of royal blood, an enormously wealthy princess, who pointed out that everybody born in Kuwait is immediately wealthy because of the nature of the country and the money they already have.

This particular princess had been married twice. Both husbands died. Both husbands left her money. So here you have a Kuwaiti princess who started out wealthy and doubled and tripled her wealth beyond a scale any of us could relate to or understand. In fact, I saw her car collection, and she let me drive one of her cars. Whenever she wanted a car, a car dealership across the country would drive a car over to her just to say, "Do you want to drive this one?" And she'd say, "No, I don't like that color." And they'd drive it back to go bring another color over. This is a woman who most people would think doesn't need to win the lottery. She's already won the lottery of life. Most people assume she has no money worries at all.

She pulled me aside and said, "Dr. Joe, I want to hire you as a coach."

I was surprised. I asked, "Well, what do you want help with?"

She said, "Money."

"How can you possibly need help with money?"

"I'm constantly in fear of people taking advantage of me," she explained. "I am constantly in fear of making a mistake with my money and making a bad investment or a bad purchase, or wasting it in some way, or looking like a fool."

Her mindset was on the other side of money. She didn't fear not having it; she feared losing it. Instead of thinking, "Oh, I need to have money because I'm limited, so I need to win the lottery," she had all the money in the world, but money was still the problem! It all goes back to mindset.

Have the mindset of expecting miracles. Take action on your dreams and make time every day, individually or with a group, to reconnect to Spirit, to Source. This is a practical spirituality. What I want is for you to walk with a sense of awakening as you go through life, awakening to the divine within yourself and all around you.

As you get into this work, you begin to realize that the whole world is alive. You begin to realize that there are synchronicities always going on, but we've been unconscious to them. We've been blind to them. We take them for granted because we don't even notice them.

I want you to consider that life is actually on your side, that you are *already* in the flow. That everything that is happening for you is for your good, for your awakening, for your spirituality.

NEXT STEPS

We've laid the foundation of a life of zero limits living. We've generated momentum. We have started the flywheel. What can you do to keep moving forward?

Well, the first pillar tells us we have to continuously awaken to what our own limitations are. That's where we work on mindset.

The second pillar tells us we must take continuous inspired action. That's where we focus on movement.

And the third pillar offers us the connection to the divine that a life of zero limits requires. That's where we discover mysticism.

Those three pillars will help you in all aspects of your life.

But.

But life happens. Death. Illness. World events. Or even just social media. Our attention gets yanked around. And as we start this journey of transformation using the three pillars of zero limits living approach, frustrations and disappointments can still crop up. What will you do when you face disappointment or apparent setbacks? Sometimes we need company on the road of life.

This is why I, even with all I have done in my career, continuously read self-help, philosophy, metaphysics, and psychology books, and still hire coaches and mentors as needed. The reason? Doing anything all by myself is entirely possible and doable, but it's generally pretty darn slow. It's not wise or fast. We need to constantly improve, grow, and expand. Life is about awakening, and that's what we're here to do.

HOW CAN YOU CONTINUOUSLY WORK ON THE THREE PILLARS?

For working on mindset, start paying attention to what your beliefs are. What is the voice in your head saying? Narrate it, write it down, become an observer to it, because you will realize you're not that voice, and some of what you're telling yourself is not helping you awaken. It's helping you stay closed.

Next, realize what you want—your intention—and take inspired, continuous action, always refining the results so you understand there's no failure. It's all feedback. We've talked about some ways to do that in the chapter on the second pillar.

And for mysticism, practice meditation. Practice gratitude. Practice sitting and looking for the quiet behind your thoughts, for the "sky" behind your thinking, for the peace behind the busyness. I've always considered the greatest and most powerful meditation to be the one where your practice is to merge with the "Witness" behind your thoughts, emotions, and body. The more you can identity with the "I of you," the more you enter the world of mysticism.

USE THE THIRD MIND

A powerful way to get accelerated results is to work in a group. One of the greatest discoveries that Napoleon Hill found and wrote about in *Think and Grow Rich*, *Law of Success*, and some of his other books is the power of a mastermind. That's when a group of people support each other with connection, pep talks, and encouragement, but on the deeper level they create what Napoleon Hill called a third mind.

The third mind is almost the esoteric internet. It's like a closed satellite group, connected on that invisible, mystical level as well as the physical. Of course, these days a mastermind group can meet virtually.

So, do your homework on a regular basis by yourself, but also do your homework with a group, because the group will give you more energy, more encouragement, and more accountability. The results will be faster and deeper. The awakening will come quicker. For me, the group experience is the best choice.

Bonus

YOUR BELIEFS ABOUT MONEY

Since so many people are caught up in survival and still believe in lack and limitation, I felt it important to add this bonus section. It's not about money; it's about your beliefs toward money. It's about your money mindset. May this bonus add to your awakening.

I want to share something with you that is the greatest moneymaking secret in history. Now, that's not hype; this is the truth. This has been the secret of the titans and tycoons of history, the wealthiest people of modern times, whether you think of Bill Gates or Jeff Bezos or somebody else. All of them and more have practiced this greatest moneymaking secret. That's what I want to share with you.

This is not about banking or finance or real estate or investing. This is really a spiritual, psychological, metaphysical, and practical technique. I learned this technique many decades ago. I was homeless and in poverty for ten years, and I had heard that there was a secret to attracting wealth, but I didn't believe it. Probably like you, I was critical. I was skeptical. I was angry. I was a victim. I blamed everybody else; I didn't take responsibility. Yet, I was trying to learn; I was trying to make a difference.

I wanted to be an author. And now, I *am* an author. I've written eighty-some books, including popular books like *The Attractor Factor, Zero Limits, At Zero, Life's Missing Instruction Manual, Hypnotic Writing, There's a Customer Born Every Minute*, and *The Fifth Phrase*. As I've mentioned, I was also in the movie *The Secret*. I've been in several other movies since then. Further, I've created about two hundred online programs. I've been prolific, productive, and prosperous.

But when I didn't know the secret I'm going to reveal to you, life was cruel. Life was a struggle. I know what it's like to go through the dark night of the soul, a night that can last days, weeks, months, years, and in my case, decades. I know what it's like to struggle and be uncertain about the future. I know what it's like to panic, to be in so much emotional pain that I wanted to give up. If you're anywhere near those kinds of experiences and if you're struggling right now, I have good news, because the greatest moneymaking secret in history will work for you, too.

What am I talking about? What does all of this mean? All right, here's the bottom line. The greatest moneymaking secret in history, the greatest money attraction secret in history, has to do with one thing. One thing that you have to do in a particular way; one thing that when you do it, and expect returns from doing it, will always work. One thing that the richest people in history have used to make a difference to attract more money. One thing that, no matter what a person's circumstances are, no matter what their position, no matter what they're struggling with, always works.

What is it? How do you do it? How do you get the mindset for success?

The greatest moneymaking secret in history is *giving, giving, giving*. Whatever you want more of, you give that. Now, we're talking about money here, so hang on; listen to me. Don't come to some snap judgments and make sweeping conclusions when you haven't heard me out.

Giving is the greatest money-attraction secret in history. You've probably heard about tithing, or heard ministers or other people in church talk about giving. That is one form of giving. Maybe you've heard about other forms of giving, like seed money. Seed money is where you give money as a way to plant money to help it grow into crops that come back to you.

Here I'm talking about a particular form of giving. How do you give and where do you give and how do you get the return? You give wherever you've received spiritual nourishment and inspiration. Now, that could be an Uber driver, a restaurant server, the people who piloted the airplane on your last flight. It can be anybody, at any institution, any organization in any walk of life. As I implied, most people think of giving in terms of the church, which is one place to give. If you have recently received spiritual nourishment from there, that's where you would give. But I'm asking you to consider where else you receive spiritual nourishment. Where do you receive inspiration? Where do you feel a boost of motivation? Where do you feel better about yourself and about life? Who or what helps you get to that place? That's where you want to give.

I remember being in a hotel room in Chicago, and the plumber came to fix the bathroom. He was the happiest plumber, and I so loved his high vibration that I wanted to give to him, and I did, which shocked him. I have given to waiters and waitresses that made me feel like a king or said something that just inspired me or opened my heart. It does not matter who or what the place or person is.

Now, how much do you give? Give whoever feeds you spiritually at least 10 percent of your income off the top, not after taxes. You want to think prosperous, be prosperous, and attract prosperity, so begin by acting prosperous. You can give it anonymously or let them see you giving it.

However you give it, do not expect a return from that person, place, or thing. If you've given 10 percent of your income to whoever it happened to be—a speaker, or a cab driver, or a store clerk who was bubbly and smiling and made you feel great and more inspired—if you gave your money there, don't expect it back from the same source. Sometimes it might, sometimes it will—miracles happen all the time—but don't expect it. Expect return, but allow the universe to surprise you. Give freely, give openly, but give with no expectation of return.

Your return of giving will come from the universe, from the cosmos, from the world, from God, from the divine, from the Great Something. Everybody has a word for this energy vortex. Deepak Chopra said it was the field of all possibilities. Napoleon Hill called it Infinite Intelligence. I sometimes call it the divine. On my last music album, I called it *The Great Something*. The Great Something will arrange for you to receive ten times (the number mentioned throughout biblical and spiritual literature) or even more of what you've given, most likely in some sort of unexpected, surprising way, some way that you will joyously celebrate when it happens. But again, don't expect it to come back from the place where you gave.

Now, people often say, "I've tried it before, but it didn't work," and I ask them, "What do you believe about money and about this karmic marketing kind of giving?" Very often, I'll find out they don't really like money; they really believe money is the root of all evil. Well, money is not the root of all evil. The lack of money is the root of all evil. Money is nothing but a means of exchange. It's simply energy, that's it. We've agreed to use this thing we call money rather than the old bartering system. Rather than me giving you a goat and you giving me a new jacket, we decide on the prices of things and we exchange money for goods and services. When you make peace with money, you can allow money to come in.

Now, in the early days, when I first tried this karmic marketing, I noticed that it didn't come back right away, or it came back in just a little bit. I had to ask myself, "What do I believe about money? What do I believe about me deserving good things?" I had to do a kind of self-coaching. Since then, I have found that having a coach is the way to have breakthroughs and accelerate the results you want. But until you hire a coach, you have to do the inner work yourself. You look in the mirror and ask yourself, "What do I believe about money?" You're exploring your mindset (the first pillar, remember).

Most people don't really like money. Most people think money is bad or it's not spiritual. You have to look at that again, because money is innocent. That's like picking up a pen and saying the pen's bad. Well, you can use a pen to stab somebody, or you can use a pen to write the great American novel. It's not the pen, it's the person using it. It's not money, it's the person using money. Make peace with money and deservingness, and you will allow it to come back to you.

Why does this principle actually work? Because money needs to circulate. What most people do—and I get this, because I did it for the longest time when I was struggling—is hold on to money. We clamp down, stuff it in our pocket, stick it in our mattress, put it in the bank, or spend it, get rid of it. We don't actually respect it; we don't actually appreciate it.

One of my favorite quotes is from Arnold Patent, who said, "The sole purpose of money is to express appreciation." When you integrate that quote alone, and just that quote by itself, you can have money, because you'll appreciate money. The sole purpose of money is to express appreciation. That means when you're writing the phone bill, don't you appreciate having a phone? When you're swiping a bank card for the groceries, don't you appreciate having groceries? When you're sending a check or wire for a car payment or house payment, don't you appreciate having a car or house? Instead of complaining about needing money, appreciate what the money is giving you.

When you do all of this in your mind, you start to make peace with money. When you give 10 percent of your money to where you receive spiritual nourishment, you've entered a field of circulation. The money goes into that circulation, travels around the world, picks up speed and more money, and comes back to you.

Now, I don't ask you to take this on faith from me. Go and try it. Put your toe in the water. Start giving. Just pay attention to how you feel. If you feel really good, if you went to a shop and you were going to buy something and the person there didn't care if you bought or not—they were just happy and they made you feel happy—that's where you want to give money. That's where you want to acknowledge the spiritual and inspirational nourishment that you got.

Once you do, *then* expect return, but not from that person. Expect return from the universe, from the Great Something, from the cosmos, from your unconscious mind, whatever you want to call it—whatever helps you understand that this formula and this system actually work.

It works for everybody. In fact, a while back, I made a video and posted it on social media. It began with me saying, "I can predict whether you're going to be rich or not." I then said, "I can predict it by asking one question, and that one question is, are you giving? Are you giving freely, generously, on a regular, consistent basis? If you are, you're probably already wealthy. If you've only begun it, you will be wealthy. Just be open, keep your heart open, make peace with money, know that you deserve good things, including wealth and great potential and the possibilities that come from being a steward for great wealth, and it will come to you."

That is the greatest moneymaking secret in history.

ILLUMINATION VIDEO TRANSCRIPTS

One of the most popular features of the online event I held that gave birth to this book was what I called "illuminations." They were eye-opening sessions to help people awaken to their limits and then transcend them. I'm sharing the transcripts here to help you further understand zero limits living. Keep in mind that these sessions were designed for people to follow online, rather than reading them. One thing you can do is record these sessions in your own voice, and then play them back. The Illuminations and Bonuses are available as online video at https://www.drjoevitalezerolimits.com/3pillars-cb.

CONTENTS

1. ILLUMINATION— CREATE YOUR REALITY

Welcome to the Zero Limits Illumination experience. In this one, we're going to consciously create your reality. To start with, you should think of what you would like to have, do, or be, and what would you welcome into your life. Now, whenever you watch or listen to this illumination, you can always change your desire and your intention as you deem fit. For now, pick something, anything—big or small, believable or a stretch—this is entirely up to you. When you live from zero limits, anything is possible, because there are no limits for you.

Therefore, what would you like to have, do, or be? Whatever comes to your mind is perfectly okay; you can make a mental note and then let it be. On the other hand, we should also focus on you relaxing and getting enough rest. Just as it has always been with these Zero Limits Illuminations, you need to be sure that you're in a place where you will not be interrupted. Neither should you be distracted, nor your attention diverted.

There is no other time than now for you to relax; it's your time to heal, your time to get clear, and to create your own reality the way you want it. So, relax into wherever you're sitting or lying. Allow the structure to support you, as you don't have to do anything. It will hold you; you can let go. You can also relax more deeply now or whenever you like. More deeply, easing away, allowing your body to let go. There's nothing to do and nowhere to go; you can follow your breathing slowly, evenly, riding your breath with your awareness, going within your body. When you exhale, you can ride the breath out with your awareness, and in and out, you let go. You relax. You're at peace.

Your mind might have many things going on, or maybe only the sound of my voice. As you know, the world is a miracle, and you are part of the world. When you live from zero limits, anything is possible, simply because there are no limits. When you come from zero, the place within, there are no boundaries, there are no rules, there are no objections, there are no limits. Whatever you want, you can have it. So, as you relax and as you breathe deeply in and out, you have the understanding that what you imagine and what you feel, you will tend to create.

Think of your intention, the one you came up with when we began. What is it that you would like to have, do, or be? Now, imagine that those intentions came true earlier today. Let a smile form on your face and a sense of awe enter your whole being as you realize your intention came through—magically, unexpectedly, but it came true. What does it feel like to have your intention already created? Imagine you are living the life of this person with this intention. The intention isn't off in the future. It already happened. Feel it real. Feel it now.

Since your intention was manifested earlier, you're so excited that you have to tell somebody. Who do you call? Imagine that you get on the phone with this person and you excitedly tell them how you manifested your own reality. Or, who do you write? Imagine that you send a text or an email or a letter describing the accomplishment, the attraction of this desire that you created. Imagine you write in your journal or your diary, or in some way you document the amazing experience of creating this reality. It came true. What does it feel like right now to have your intention manifested?

Feel it—allow the emotions of happiness, euphoria, serenity, pride to all swell in and around your body. Feel it all right now. Relish the experience of having created somehow, some way, your intention. It feels wonderful. Now allow every one of your feelings to wander off, floating away from you out into the universe in a way such that your desire and all the feelings, all the imagery, float into zero. Sense or even pretend that your desire that has been fulfilled has gone into zero, and at zero, it can become reality in your third-dimensional world.

This particular zero limit illumination proves that anything is possible. Miracles are real. You are one with zero and you deserve all good things, including your intentions. Now, bring your attention back to the room you're in, back to your body, back to this present moment. You're welcome to go to sleep if you like; you're welcome to get up refreshed, happy, relaxed, and confident, knowing you have created your own reality.

2. ILLUMINATION—BLOCKS TO HAVING MORE BUSINESS

Now, in this Zero Limits Illumination, we will clear all the blocks there are to having more business. Business, as you know, is good. Business is an extension of your life calling, your life mission, and your soul's purpose. Making peace with business, making peace with money, making peace with success, all enables you to have more, do more, and be more. You and your business can make a difference in the world where it is needed most.

Therefore, for this Zero Limits Illumination, as usual, relax. Be sure you won't be interrupted: there won't be distractions or disturbances. These few minutes together are precious and priceless. This is your time, your time to get clear, to cleanse, to heal, to open yourself to business prosperity. The more you receive through your business, the more people you touch, the more people you influence, the more you, your family, friends, and community all prosper.

As you relax, you should pay attention to your breathing. You can even slow it down if you like. Breathing slowly in and slowly out, slowly in and slowly out. You might even imagine your breath to be a color, a color that comes to mind for you, and visualize breathing in this color, filling your whole body with it, and when you release, imagine that this color is bathing you, cleansing you, healing you, and protecting you. Breathe in this color, and let it go all the way through the inside of you, coloring your entire inside of your body. By the time you release it, let the color surround you, creating an aura of business prosperity.

You can as well breathe in another color if you like, any color that comes to mind, knowing that these colors are coming from your connection to zero. Trust them. You can breathe the color out and breathe the color back in. It feels good to let go and relax. Now imagine another color that you breathe in. Any color that comes to mind is fine. They're all good. They all heal. They all clear and cleanse.

Breathe that color in and breathe that color out. This easy, natural rhythm relaxes and eases you. Ensure you let the colors go as you relax, continue your gentle breathing, and imagine your business. Allow whatever vision comes to mind; it could be you, it could be the name of your business, it could be the logo, it could be your website, it could be your products or services. Whatever comes to mind is fine; allow it.

As you sit with this image of your business, see it surrounded by white light. The white light that signifies protection, security, prosperity, opulence. The white light that cleanses you and your business to allow more. You could imagine breathing in the white light if you like, and you could also imagine breathing out the white light if you like. This white light focused on your business makes it shine. There's a glow on the image that you see, maybe a glow you feel.

You could imagine your business increasing in prosperity, easily, naturally, organically. You may not know how, but you can sense it's happening, and it's happening for the highest good of all concerned. As you relax and let go, let this white light heal you in your relationship to your business. You can also imagine the white light expands to touch other people in the world, your customers, your clients, your prospects. This white light extends from you and your business reaching out with rays of light, around the entire planet, touching people in places that awaken their interest in your services.

See this white light extending from you and your business and saturating the planet itself. Planet Earth has a glow of white light, an aura of prosperity, all stemming from you and your business. It all begins at the center point zero. Zero is at your core and, at zero, anything is possible. Therefore, from the zero within you, the white light exudes, enlarges, expands, and blankets the entire planet, touching millions of people. Your wealth, your prosperity, your business success, it all comes from other people. Your aura, your vibration is increasing naturally and easily and reaching more people around the planet.

Every time you do this Zero Limits Illumination, your reach extends even further, even deeper, even more permanently. You know your business is a spiritual force for good. You deserve success. Your business deserves success. Now, allow those vibrations and images to disappear. Let them go from your consciousness. Let them go back to zero where they will be planted as seeds and grow into an enormous business prosperity tree. You're back in your environment in real time, feeling happy, healthy, rejuvenated, and even more prosperous. If you'd like to go to sleep, you can, or you can stay awake, eyes bright, expecting miracles.

3. ILLUMINATION—YOUR HEALTH

As you know, at zero, anything is possible. Zero limits living means living where there are no limitations and anything is possible. There are no restrictions, no boundaries, no impossibilities, and this is true for everything, including your health.

Therefore, let's begin by doing something very healthy: relaxing. Many studies have proven that, by simply relaxing, you will be healed and even cured of numerous health-oriented problems. So, let's begin here. Relax. Ordinarily, just by saying the word relax, it helps you relax, and sometimes following your breathing, putting your awareness on your breath, and watching it as it goes in your body and out your body can help bring you into the moment, and can also help bring you into the present time.

This moment is the miracle. In this moment, all is well. It's our mind that makes us think otherwise. It's our judgments of right or wrong, good and bad, that cause us conflict, that cause us our unhappiness and our unhealthy conditions. As you're breathing, allow the breath to bring you into this moment. Feel your body, wiggle your toes, move your fingers, shake your hands, fidget a little bit, to find that place of comfort where your body relaxes.

It helps that for the next few minutes, you know you're neither going to be interrupted nor disturbed. You're in a safe environment, where it's just you and me, and I'm speaking to the deepest aspects of you, going past the conscious, deeper than the subconscious, and beyond the unconscious, all the way to the point of zero. Miracles occur at zero. This moment is a miracle. Your life, your breathing, your consciousness, is all a gift.

As you're breathing and relaxing, focus on what you appreciate about your body. What are you grateful for? It could be your heart pumping, it could be your lungs breathing, it could be your blood traveling through your body. It could be your muscles that are holding you, yet relaxing with you. It could be your bones that are holding you up and together. It could be your brain and all that it does to help you function and be alive. It could be your eyes. It could be your hearing, which enables you to follow my voice and relax even more.

From breathing to living, sleeping, eating, digesting, and so much more, what are you grateful for? When you think of your body, what is it that is working that you love so much? For a moment, just focus on the thing or things that you love about your body that work. Whatever you focus on expands. If you feel good and you feel grateful about one aspect of your body, you will realize that such a sense of gratefulness can expand to other areas and awaken them to heal, to cure, and to become whole again.

As you're breathing and relaxing, imagine a butterfly flies into your awareness. Pretend that it's around you, fluttering, beautiful. It seems mystical; it may be extra special in some way. But as you're relaxing, this beautiful, mystical, colorful butterfly is just playing touch and go with your body, and wherever it seems to touch, there's a healing. There's an illumination. There's a little bit of soft energy that's transmitted from the butterfly to you.

Even if the butterfly just flies all around you, there seems to be an awakening of healing consciousness, and your sails seem to dance and come alive. Your body begins to rejuvenate and all the aspects of your body that you love are intensified and beautified, and the parts that you want to be healed begin to awaken to healing. This beautiful butterfly does a few circles around you, it seems to be there just for you, and then flies off; you are now letting it go, relaxing as you go into your natural healing now.

As you're breathing and relaxing and feeling your body, healthy and becoming healthier, you appreciate your body. You are grateful for your body, as your body enables you to enjoy the life experience. As your body and mind get better and better, you enjoy your life more and more. The more grateful you are for what is working in your body, the more your body begins to work entirely, all aspects awakening with the illumination that anything is possible with belief, with faith, with returning to zero.

Zero, the home of zero limits. Zero limits living is zero limits health. Health and well-being are yours at zero limits. Now, as you relax and you focus on your breathing and you hear my voice, you can return your awareness to the room you're in, to present reality, and if you want to go to sleep, you can do so, drifting into a deep, restful, healing sleep. Perhaps, you want to stay awakened, knowing that you feel better, that you are healing, that you are becoming all that you wish to be, because with Zero Limits Illumination, your healing is now and you are grateful.

4. ILLUMINATION— RELATIONSHIPS

In this Zero Limits Illumination, you and I will focus on relationships. In zero limits, we understand that all relationships are projections of our relationship with our very own self. That being said, the very first thing we need to do is make peace with ourselves. The next thing we do after that is to realize all relationships are based on love. When we reconnect to our love, we reconnect to the wisdom of interpersonal peace. Therefore, to begin with, be sure you won't be interrupted for the next few minutes, and relax. No distractions, and absolutely nothing to do. This is your time to heal, to relax, to cleanse, to clear, to reach an awakening in terms of relationship.

Now, I'm speaking to your subconscious, unconscious, and conscious to create a relationship of mutual respect and peace with yourself and with all of life.

Zero Limits Illumination is the realization that you are one with all. As you breathe slowly and evenly, you will notice you relax easily. The stories I tell, the language I use, are to speak to a deeper aspect of you. Your mind may not be able to follow, but your heart will open. As you relax and let go, your body eases, allowing yourself to be supported by whatever you are sitting or lying on. Gradually, as you attain this inner tranquility, all that needs to be done is for you to let go, to find that inner peace that has been there all along.

Whatever relationship you came to this moment thinking about, be reminded of the wisdom that the only relationship you have is with yourself. As you love yourself and appreciate yourself, that respect vibrates out to touch all of the relationships you have. All relationships are with you. A disruption in any relationship is simply a reflection of a little bump in your relationship with yourself. But as you go through the Zero Limits Illuminations, you find peace. You re-merge with the state of zero; you connect to that space of unlimited possibilities and potential. Also, you realize at the center of you there is love, and that love in you reaches out and touches anyone and everyone from whom you at one time felt separate. In Zero Limits Illuminations, you realize all of life is one divine energy. It's all love. It's all good.

So, as you relax, allowing your breathing to make you even more comfortable and at ease, allowing your mind to relax, a gentler peace seems to envelop your entire body, causing you to be at ease with everyone and everything. Enlightenment is when you realize we are all one. You can open your inner arms and your inner heart to allow, receive, and accept everything. At zero, all is well.

If you felt that there was an issue with somebody, bring that person and that issue into this inner light and allow the love in you to wash it clean. You're simply reconnecting with yourself. The old way of looking at the world was looking with separation. The new way is to look with inclusion. Zero limits is all about awakening, realizing you and the others have always been one being of light. This Zero Limits Illumination creates the awareness that is beyond all understanding. It brings you to that sense of peace beyond all understanding. All relationships can be smooth, easy, loving, respectful. Reminding yourself of that fact will make life smooth.

Now, as you breathe and relax and look within, you realize judgments create divisions. And so you release the judgments so you can receive all people, all relationships, allowing them to stem from the inner you. You are one; the divine lives and breathes through you. And the divine does not judge. The divine loves. The divine loves all; the divine loves you.

And now, as you relax into the awareness that all is peace and love, you can roll over and go to sleep, or you can stretch and awaken. In either case, you will feel whole, complete, loved, and lovable, and you will live from the place of zero limits with wisdom, grace, and gratitude.

5. ILLUMINATION—
PEACE WITH YOURSELF

In this Zero Limits Illumination, I'm going to lead you into making peace with yourself. Now, as with all of these illuminations, be sure you're in a place where you will not be interrupted. Turn off your phone; close your door. This is your time. This is for you to relax, to cleanse, to clear, to heal. It's your time to make peace with you. So just relax. You can sit; you can lie down. It's entirely up to you how deeply you relax now. I'll be speaking to your conscious mind, your subconscious mind, and your unconscious mind. You can listen to my voice or not. You can let your mind wander if you like. You will still have the illumination of making peace with yourself. And the more you listen or watch this illumination, the more you will relax, the more you will be at peace.

So, again, just relax. Breathe deep, and follow your breathing into your body. And when you release it, follow it out. Let your awareness ride your breathing. Feels good to relax. As your breathing slows and becomes gentle and is already relaxing, allow your body to relax. Whether you're sitting or prone, imagine that, wherever you are, it's supporting you. It's holding you. You don't have to work. You don't have to try. You are being supported. And metaphysically you're being supported in your life. You are loved. You are cared for. You are one with all that is. You are one with the divine, one with the cosmos.

As you breathe, as you relax, whisper to your body to let go. Maybe imagine your toes relaxing—wiggle them a little bit—your fingers relaxing. And allow this gentle wave of relaxation to go all the way through your body, traveling up your arms, traveling up your legs. It's good to let go. You may feel a slight tingling as you let go. You may feel nothing but serenity. As you let go, you realize just how grateful you are to be alive, to have the ability to breathe, to have a body to carry you through life, to have a heartbeat, to have a mind, to have a soul. As you realize just how grateful you are, you relax even more. And maybe a smile forms on your face as you realize the peace you seek is the peace within. All that is, is in you. You are one with the power, with the spirit, with all potential. Inside you, deep within, there's a calmness, a serenity. There's no problems, no challenges, no issues, no negativity. Inside you, beyond the illusion of concerns, sits peace, calmness, tranquility.

You should breathe deeply and evenly and repeatedly. You become one with this peace. The peace beyond all understanding. This peace inside you, beyond your mind, behind all concerns. This peace is always there, always waiting, ready, willing, patient, for you to become aware of it and to merge with it. Your illumination is the understanding that this peace is always with you. Whenever you take a moment and relax, and breathe, and look within, you can sense that serenity. There's nothing for you to do. There's nothing for you to change. At the core, you are whole. You are total. You are complete. You are enough. You are loved.

Feel that love deep within you. Breathe into it. Let that love expand through your entire body. Let that love bring you peace. Let that love fill every part of you, all the way through and around you. You have peace. You are love. You are loved.

You can access this illumination of peace by just pausing, breathing, reminding yourself that it's there, always available. And now feel this peace for a moment.

If you want to fall asleep, you can. If you want to stretch and bring yourself into present reality, you can. Know that this inner peace is always available. This peace with yourself, this connection to the peace of the universe, is right there within you.

You have been illuminated to the reality of peace beyond all understanding with yourself. Relax and sleep or relax and awaken—it's entirely up to you. And you feel wonderful, refreshed, rejuvenated with a sense of calm serenity and total peace with yourself.

6. ILLUMINATION—MONEY

In this Zero Limits Illumination, we'll address the subject of money. As you know, at zero, there are no judgments, there are no limits, there are no boundaries. You can virtually do, be, or have anything you want and anything you can imagine, including more money. At zero, money is neutral. Nobody is condemning it, nobody is resisting it, nobody is avoiding it. Money in and of itself is nothing but energy. You are energy and you can attract even more energy in any forms that you can imagine, including money. So, now, for this Zero Limits Illumination, just relax. I'm speaking to your conscious, subconscious, unconscious, and the spiritual aspect of the collective unconscious. You don't need to follow along, you don't need to take notes, you can let go. Trust; have faith.

And as usual, be sure that you are in a comfortable, uninterrupted environment. There's nothing for you to do, nowhere for you to go. This is your time—your time to merge with the energy of money and enlarge that vibration to magnetize yourself to receive unlimited funds and all forms of money. So follow your breathing as it comes in and follow it with your awareness as it drifts out, a nice, easy, gentle process, natural, relaxing.

And as you relax, you can reflect on all the good things you can do with money. You can certainly help yourself, family, friends, community, causes you believe in. Money is a spiritual tool for good. The sole purpose of money is to express appreciation. You respect money, you have a healthy relationship with money, you are grateful for money. Money allows you to fulfill your dreams, your calling, your life mission. Money enables you to help people, including yourself. Because there's an unlimited supply of money, you are comfortable giving it away, investing it, purchasing what is important to you, saving it, building with it, sharing it.

As you wisely steward money, you enter the circulation of money. Knowing money comes to you, you disperse it in wise ways, and money comes back to you many times more in unexpected ways, and you are grateful. As you open your heart to receive more money, you know that you can do more good with more money. As you relax, as your breathing is slow and easy, imagine that inside of you is a magnet, a very strong magnet that attracts good things, including money.

And as you visualize this magnet within you, feel it vibrate. It has a little shimmer, a little dance of energy that you can feel, that you can sense, and as it vibrates and dances within you, you can sense that this is spinning and pulling in more money to you. And as this money comes to you, you are free to direct it wherever you want it to go. Money comes to you in surprising ways, unexpected ways, ways that make you joyous, happy, ways that make you celebrate, ways that make you feel good about yourself and your mission in life. The more money you receive, the more good you can do with it.

And as this inner vibration spins and enlarges and becomes even more powerful, it vibrates throughout your body and vibrates into the aura of energy around you. It feels good, and for a moment, just feel that vibration, pulling energy, attracting energy, bringing money to you, and your heart is open and your arms are wide, knowing money is a force for good. You will use it wisely; you are grateful for it.

And as you breathe and relax, a little smile forms on your face, knowing this is all benevolent, this is all good. And perhaps you can see yourself sharing money with people and causes that you believe in, that you care about, and you enjoy it for yourself as well. You are worthy, you are good enough, and you deserve good things, too. And now, as the image of the vibration and the magnet begin to disappear, the feelings of goodness and spiritual awakening remain. You're reminded that, at zero, anything is possible. This Zero Limits Illumination proves that you can have anything, including money.

There are no limits; there are no restrictions. As you open your mind and open your heart, you open yourself to receive more—more good, more wealth, more prosperity, more money. And now, bring your attention back to the room that you're in, back to present reality. If you want to go to sleep, you can. If you want to open your eyes and awaken and be refreshed, knowing profound changes have taken place on a deep level, you can do that, too. And every time you read this Zero Limits Illumination, you will more quickly and deeply and profoundly relax and more deeply and profoundly open yourself to receive more money.

7. ILLUMINATION— LEAD YOU TO ZERO

In this Zero Limits Illumination, I'm going to lead you to zero. I'm going to help you connect to the divine. Now, with all of these illuminations, be sure that you're not going to be interrupted. Turn off your phone, block your door, be in a safe environment without any distractions, without any potential interruptions. This is your time. This is your time to relax. This is your time to heal, to clear, to cleanse, to let go.

So get comfortable. You can sit, you can lie down. It's entirely up to you. And whether you sit or lie down, allow what you're on to support you, to hold you. You don't have to struggle; you don't have to strain. Let go, trust, have faith. So, as you settle in to whatever position feels really good to you, just take in a deep breath, hold it a second, and release it, letting go. You can do it again: take in a deep breath, hold it a second, release it. It feels good. Allow your breathing to be easy and slow and even. You're relaxing; it's so good to relax. It feels good to let go. All the stresses just fall away. You ease as your body melts.

And you can watch your breathing, ride the breath in, feel it go inside you, and ride the breath out with your awareness.

Now, as you're relaxing, following your breathing, notice that you're having thoughts. Your mind is still active and that's okay, but as your mind is still active, thinking and wondering, notice that you are not your mind. You can observe your thoughts, you can report on your thoughts, which suggests that you are not your thoughts. You are separate from your thoughts. Thoughts may come and go, but you, witnessing them, you are always there. And notice your body—you may be relaxed and relaxing. You may need to move a little bit to be more comfortable. Notice you have a body and somehow you can report on that body and tell me or anyone how you feel.

Somehow you are a witness to your body. You're separate from it. You're detached from your body. The body is something you wear. You are within it, but you are not your body. And now, notice your emotions. Maybe you're happy, sad, curious. You can have any number of emotions coming and going, always changing, but you, the observer of those emotions, always remain the same. You are not your emotions. You are separate from your emotions. And now, consider, if you are not your thoughts and you are not your body and you are not your emotions, what are you? Who are you? The part of you that can witness thoughts and witness your body and witness your emotions is zero.

It is the background essence of your life. That background observer, we can call zero, and the further illumination is the reality that this zero in you is the same zero in me, and the same zero in everyone. Behind all of our thoughts, behind all of our bodies, behind all of our emotions is this aware witness, this spiritual observer that we can call zero. Zero is alive, zero is intelligent, zero can live and breathe through you. Whenever you watch or listen to this particular illumination, it will bring you to zero. Zero is always available, zero is peace, zero is tranquility.

8. BONUS—BRAIN COMMANDS

In this section we want to talk about brain commands. And I want to give you seven daily brain commands that you can go ahead and implement. You can do one of these a day or you can do them all each day for seven days. And of course you can recycle this and keep doing it for seven weeks, seven months, seven years, as much as you like. What we're talking about is giving commands to your own brain. Now, your brain is already pre-wired for survival. And so your mind is on alert for anything that could be a threat to your existence, and that's good. It's also good that it's working because you're here, you're watching me, and I'm here making this for you.

Our pre-wired system is alive and well and working wonderfully, but what most people don't know is you can also wire your brain to do other things. For example, to bring you wealth, to bring you health, to bring you happiness, to bring you spirituality, to help you in any way, shape, or form that you can imagine.

Now I want to give you a very, very simple thing to do. Simple but profound. To program your mind with these brain commands, you need to understand that what we're doing is giving a very short, positive declarative order to your mind. You're telling it something to do. Now, in some circles, they call these affirmations. Remember my earlier story? I had lunch with a woman years ago and she said, "Oh, I tried affirmations, and affirmations don't work for me." And I looked at her and I said, "Do you realize the statement 'Affirmations don't work for me' is an affirmation? You're affirming that they don't work, then you're getting the result that they don't seem to work because you affirmed that they don't work. Do you follow?"

Affirmations do work. And they work whether you are stating a positive intent or a negative intent. So, what we want to do is take control and point ourselves in the positive direction of life. Isn't that where you want to go? That's where I want to go. I came up with seven affirmations. There's lots of them all over the internet that you can search for. You can pick and choose which ones you want. But these seven plus a bonus one are the ones that I think you should begin with right now. You can expand later. What are they?

The first one is "Anything is possible." I so love this statement that I wrote a book called *Anything Is Possible*. That's because a lot of us think that some things can't be changed—the circumstances can't be changed, or our lives can't be changed. We think things are set in stone or ourselves or our family are set in stone. And we don't realize that, no, everything is pretty much plastic. It's moldable. If you have an affirmation that says, "Anything is possible," it opens your mind to look for other possibilities, other solutions, other choices, other options. It's a very empowering place to be. You're certainly not a victim. If you think anything is possible, you are now empowered. You're now more of a victor. You are more in control of your life.

As I said, you can do one of these affirmations a day and, whenever you think of it, just look at it. One thing you can do is write the affirmation on a card, such as a business card. You can write "Anything is possible" on your business card and put it in your pocket. And then whenever your hand goes into your pocket or your wallet or your purse, you will touch it. And just touching the affirmation will trigger your brain to remember it.

The second affirmation is "There is always a way." This has been something that I have used for my biggest successes in life, because instead of thinking, "Well, I hit a roadblock. I can't accomplish something that I want. I might as well give up on my goal. I'm not going to attract it or achieve it," instead I think, "There is always a way." Even when I feel like I'm backed into a corner, like the world's descending on me, that the clouds aren't going to break, I think, "There is always a way." Just having the belief "There is always a way."

It's an affirmation. It's a brain command. It opens my mind to look and ask, where's the way? It either exists and somebody else already did it, or I need to find a way or create a way to resolve this problem. Whatever it happens to be, if you have the brain command "There is always a way," you'll keep looking. You won't give up and, beautifully, you'll find a way, or create a way, or find somebody who can create it for you, or find somebody who's already done it.

The third affirmation is a biggie: "I deserve success." By now, you know I've written a lot of books, including *Money Loves Speed*, *The Awakened Millionaire*, and *Attract Money Now*, where I talk about how the idea of deserving something is one of the biggest blocks for people, whether they're trying to attract money or success or more sales or a relationship. Sometimes the block to attracting and achieving what they want is an internal belief that they don't deserve success. They feel like they're not worthy. At first, with the brain command "I deserve success," you have to repeat it, because you're giving yourself a new programming, a new self-talk. But as you repeat it, it begins to take hold. It becomes a new wiring. It becomes a new programming, and soon it becomes your new reality.

The fourth is another important one: "I am safe." So many of us are afraid, and because of that fear, we don't take any action. We stay in our comfort zone and we want to live with a blanket over us because we're afraid of life. We're afraid of judgment. We're afraid of failure. We're afraid of criticism. We're just afraid, period, and, of course, being afraid ties into what I began all of this talking about, and that's the idea of survival. And because we want to survive, a part of us keeps us in check until we realize that we are already safe.

I've said many times that a good goal or a good intention is something that scares you a little bit and excites you a lot because it moves you. It nudges you right out of your comfort zone. This affirmation, this brain command, "I am safe," helps you relax slightly. The reality is you're not doing anything that's death defying. What you're doing is going for dreams, whether you want more money or you want a relationship or better health. These are not death-defying things. These are not things to be afraid of. What we want to do is realize that "I am safe."

Now, the fifth brain command is "Every day in every way I am getting better and better." And this one goes all the way back to Émile Coué, a pharmacist who discovered that self-talk, positive commands, and brain commands could actually change people. And the most famous one was this one: "Every day in every way I am getting better and better."

Go ahead and say that. It feels good. In fact, I smile when I say it. Every day in every way I'm getting better and better. That is just a positive brain command that tells your body and mind system to keep moving forward in a positive way.

The sixth one is "I am good enough." And what that means is I'm complete the way I am. So many of us, much like in the affirmation "I deserve success," feel that we don't deserve success because we don't feel like we're good enough. We feel like we're lacking in some way. And the truth is you're not lacking in any way. I was homeless. I was in poverty. I did poorly in school. I did poorly in college. I didn't graduate when I initially went to college—I felt stupid, so I felt I was lacking. And then, of course, being homeless, I felt like I had no self-esteem. But the reality is, I *am* good enough and I *am* safe and I *do* deserve success, and look at me now. If I can do it, you can do it, too.

"I am good enough" is the statement to help your brain and your mind relax into realizing you don't have to do anything in particular to deserve success. You are good enough as you are. Now, of course, you're going to grow. You're going to morph into more and you're going to be reaching and stretching. But as you are, you're still good enough.

The seventh one is another biggie: "I forgive myself and others." Forgiveness is one of the biggies in life. I think it was Wayne Dyer who said, "If there's a block anywhere in your life, it's due to a lack of forgiveness." You want to forgive yourself. You want to forgive everybody else. When you hold on to grudges and resentments and things that bother you, you're actually burning your own system up. Your own energy is being set on fire in you. The other people that you may not have forgiven don't even feel what you're going through. You're the one who's feeling it. You have to free yourself, but how do you free yourself? Forgiveness. I forgive myself; I forgive others. Those can be two affirmations if you like, or just put them together—"I forgive myself and others"—and be free.

Those are seven. I wrote down a bonus one because I thought this was so important: "I am grateful." I truly know that the two ways to transform your life in any one moment are with forgiveness and gratitude. In several movies, I tell a famous pencil story about when I was struggling, and everybody said, "Oh, be grateful." And I said, "I'll be grateful when I have something to be grateful for." And I picked up a pencil and flippantly said, "Oh, I'll be grateful for this." And within a couple minutes of faking it, I started to actually feel grateful. You can just look around and pick up something in the moment to be grateful for. And as you move into that energy, it'll shift you.

All of this is a quick overview on affirmations. You can write your own, the kind that make you feel good when you think about them, say them, or write them. Make them short, make them positive, make them punchy, make them energetic. You can also do some googling and find books on affirmations and so forth. But I'm giving you these seven daily brain commands:

1. Anything is possible.
2. There is always a way.
3. I deserve success.
4. I am safe.
5. Every day in every way I am getting better and better.
6. I am good enough.
7. I forgive myself and others.

And the bonus, "I am grateful."

Work with those and expect miracles.

(By the way, the T-shirt I was wearing in the video version of the above said, "Kindness is invincible." It's an affirmation, two thousand years old, from Marcus Aurelius, the poster boy for Stoicism.)

9. BONUS—
SEVEN-DAY ACCELERATOR

In this bonus item, we're going to be talking about the Seven-Day Accelerator. These are suggestions on what you can do every day, one a day, for seven days, to kick-start, jump-start, and otherwise help you get moving and accelerate your path to whatever your goal or goals happen to be. I've whittled this down to very strategic methods and techniques that I myself use. So, what are they?

Day one, *what is your intention?* If you don't know what you want, nothing will happen and you won't go anyplace in particular. So, what is it you want to have, do, or be? On day one, you should really know what this is. Right now I'm asking you not only to answer the question "What do you want?" but to write it down. Writing's very important because you're programming your mind, you're programming your brain, you're telling yourself in very clear terms, "This is my goal, this is my outcome, this is my desire, this is the result." And, when your brain understands specifically what you want, it can begin working and even manipulate reality, touching the lives of other people and awakening them on a collective unconscious level, to bring you the very thing that you say you want. But it's not going to bring it if you don't say what you want. So, on day one, answer the question "What is your intention?"—what do you want to have, do, or be—and put that in writing.

Now on day two, you're going to *visualize your intention*. It's one thing to write it; writing it is very good. The reason that we have lots of contracts is they establish clarity between people. Well, the written intention creates clarity between you and your brain. You're not your brain. You get to use your brain, but you're not your brain.

So, after day one, where the written statement is a contract, on day two you will visualize this. The brain responds to imagery. This is one reason we make vision boards, as described in the mindset chapter, because imagery is how the brain responds and understands what you want. So, in order to program your mind for success, you need to be able to imprint your brain with your desire. Find (or create) graphics and images that represent the completion of what you're looking for.

Day three—and this is very important—*feel it real.* Day three is where you imagine you've actually created, achieved, and manifested what you want. So now you're feeling it. On day one you wrote it out, day two you were seeing pictures of it, and now on day three, you're feeling it. Your brain responds to emotions. Love, hate, and fear are very strong emotional activators. This is like pouring gasoline on your image and lighting it, so you want to have emotion.

The best way to do this is, first, to go back and reread your vision that you wrote on day one and see the pictures that you created on day two. Then, you're going to imagine you've already achieved your intention. You can elaborate on this by, for instance, pretending to call up your best friend, or posting it on Facebook and other social media to celebrate what you did. What would you tell your friend? What would you post? How would you celebrate the accomplishment of what you want? How would it feel? And then imagine that you are sharing this feeling. Are you with me? So, on day three you're feeling that everything's already accomplished and you're telling other people about it. You're going into an after-the-fact kind of a description.

Now, day four is something that you can do called *What If UP*. While recording this video, I was wearing a shirt called "whatifupper." I am a member of the What If UP Club. I'm the president of the club. Yes, I'm the president, and I'm a board member. What If UP is a way to "up" how you're thinking about what you want and about the possibilities of creating what you want. Mendhi Audlin explained it well in her book *What If It All Goes Right?*

What If DOWN means you've started to criticize things. "What if this doesn't work? What if this is a bomb? What if I'm a failure?" Those are all What If DOWN. When you say those kinds of statements, your energy drops—it goes down. So here, on day four, I want you to create a What If UP experience and go in the other direction—up. "What if it works? What if it's easy? What if it all happens at an accelerated rate? What if this is a breakthrough? What if this is the greatest moment of my entire life?"

Notice how those all feel better. Notice how your energy goes up. That's whatifupping.

So, on day four, I want you to imagine whatifupping everything. What if your intention becomes even better than what you originally stated? What if the images you were creating and looking at on day two are nowhere near as powerful as the images you're getting now—greater, better, more powerful? The same with day three and feeling everything. What have you actually felt so real to the degree that you don't even need it anymore because it feels like it's already happened? So, you whatifup the experience.

Day five is an advanced technique called *the remembering process*. What I want you to do is to pretend that not only did your intention come true, because you already felt it real on day three, but also that you are going into the future, past the moment of it coming true, and remembering from that point some possible things you did to manifest your intention. Daniel Barrett and I wrote a book called *The Remembering Process* that will help you more fully understand this, but for now just know the remembering process is a way for you to remember back to the creation of your intention.

Now, understand me here. On one level, your intention hasn't happened yet. We're only into day five in the Seven-Day Accelerator program, but you're imagining it already manifested yesterday, and you're imagining now you are even beyond yesterday, and you are remembering back. And like lots of memories, they're a little bit fuzzy, so you're asking yourself, how did I achieve my intention? How did I attract it? Whatever comes to mind on how you did it are clues that could be ideas, options, and opportunities that you can act on now. So, play with this a little bit. I know this step might be unusual, but these shortcuts and hacks that make up the Seven-Day Accelerator are for you to play with and to see what works and what you really like.

Day six is a reminder to *act on your ideas*: your inspirations, your hunches, your opportunities, all the things that present themselves to you. See, the number one thing people do wrong if they do all these other steps correctly is they don't take action. I'm a big take-action guy. In the movie

The Secret, I tell viewers it's your job to take action. I talk all the time about taking action. So, on day six, remember that if you have a gnawing feeling to do something, even if it doesn't make sense, you should act on it.

Here's a story I have told many times on stages around the world. When I worked for an oil company way back in the 1980s, everybody would leave at lunchtime and go eat at the mall food court. One day when I was leaving to do exactly that, something in me said, "Turn left." Now, I had never turned left. Yet something in me said, "Turn left." I could have ignored it, but it was a kind of a gnawing impulse, an inspiration, an intuitive hit, a gut feeling. It was a mystery, but I thought, I'll go ahead and do it. I turned left. Short story is, I found an Italian deli. I was so in love with the food and the man there, on my own I copied the menu, made a new menu for it, and hung it up in my office. I wanted to spread the word about my chef and his gourmet food.

And this guy, who was struggling in his Italian deli business, suddenly had lots of business. And he always remembered it. He was always grateful. And at some point when he was ready to sell his home, he gave it—his home—to my wife and me, when we were still struggling back in the 1980s . . . couldn't get a home, couldn't get credit, didn't have an established track record of success. And all that came from following my gut, my feeling. You never know where your intuitive impulses are going to take you. So, on day six, make sure that you are acting on the opportunities that come your way, even when they don't make any rational sense to you.

Last, on day seven, your task is to *go through all of these again.* Day seven is a reminder to read your intention every day, not just on day seven. It's a reminder to visualize the success of your intention every day, not just on day seven. It's also a reminder to feel the accomplishment of your intention, not just on day seven. The idea is, by doing all of this on a regular basis—and none of this is very time-consuming, though all of it should be joyful because you're doing it for something that you want—you will accelerate, which is the whole point of the Seven-Day Accelerator. You will accelerate your path to the very thing you want to manifest. This stuff works.

So, I invite you to review this if you need to. Check out more information on things like What If UP with Mendhi Audlin's book *What If It All Goes Right?*, or the remembering process with the book that Daniel and I wrote called *The Remembering Process*, and play with these tools—have fun with them. But I think the real important things are to know what you want and to take action regularly and be persistent—don't ever give up. Persistence might be the greatest unspoken, unacknowledged secret of the universe. Persistence. Expect miracles.

MORE BONUSES

Please visit
https://www.drjoevitalezerolimits.com/3pillars-cb
for other information related to *Zero Limits Living*.

SUMMARY

Welcome to the end—and the beginning.

The end of this book and the beginning of experiencing zero limits living. I hope you are inspired to embrace the three pillars: mindset, movement, and mysticism.

Remember, your mindset is the key to unlocking your full potential, so cultivate a positive and determined outlook on life. This is all about what you think.

Moving your body, even in small ways, will boost your energy and vitality, particularly if you are moving it in the direction of your chosen goals and intentions. This is all about movement. Take action in the direction of your dreams, goals, and inspirations.

Finally, mysticism reminds us that there is a greater power at work in the universe. You aren't alone and you do not need to act alone. This is all about spirituality. "The Great Something" is guiding your way, quietly, subtly, and constantly. Tune in to it.

Combine all three and you have a formula for miraculous success in all areas of your life.

But it's not enough to simply read and understand these concepts—it's time to be an inspiration to others.

Let your newfound mindset, movement, and mysticism guide you toward your dreams and aspirations. Allow your actions to be inspired and rooted in these three pillars, and watch as the world around you begins to transform.

So go forth, dear reader, and embrace the power of zero limits living. Let it guide you toward a life of fulfillment, purpose, and abundance. And remember, by embodying these pillars, you can become a beacon of inspiration and change in the world around you.

Expect Miracles!

Dr. Joe Vitale
www.MrFire.com

ACKNOWLEDGMENTS

Thanks to Mary Beth Conlee for editing the transcripts that led to this book. Thanks to Joshua Alabi for editing the Illuminations and bonuses in the back of this book. Thanks to Sean Donahoe for cohosting the original online event. Thanks to Chuck Pennington for designing the website for the event. Thanks to my love, Lisa Winston, for feeding and watering me while I produced this material. Thanks to my team behind Miracles Coaching®. Thanks of course to Matt Holt and his team at Matt Holt Books, an imprint of Ben-Bella Books, for turning this material into a beautiful book to help the world. I am grateful to all.

BIBLIOGRAPHY

Atkinson, William Walter. *Thought Vibration, or The Law of Attraction in the Thought World.* Chicago: New Thought Publishing, 1906.

Audlin, Mendhi. *What If It All Goes Right? Creating a New World of Peace, Prosperity & Possibility* Garden City, NY: Morgan James Publishing, 2010.

Barret, Daniel, and Joe Vitale. *The Remembering Process.* Carlsbad, CA: Hay House, 2015.

Beauregard, Mario, and Denyse O'Leary. *The Spiritual Brain: A Neuroscientist's Case for the Existence of the Soul.* HarperOne, 2007.

Fox, Emmet. *The Mental Equivalent.* Life Summit, MO: Unity, 1932.

Goddard, Neville. *Neville Goddard Lecture Series*. 12 vols. Albuquerque: Audio Enlightenment Press, 2014.

Hardy, Benjamin. *Personality Isn't Permanent*. New York: Portfolio, 2020.

Hartong, Leo. *Awakening to the Dream: The Gift of Lucid Living*. Oakland, CA: Non-Duality, 2003.

Hill, Napoleon. *Think and Grow Rich*. New York: Fawcett Books, 1935.

James, William. *The Principles of Psychology*. New York: H. Holt and Company, 1890.

Larson, Christian D. *Just Be Glad*. Los Angeles: The New Literature Publishing Company, 1912.

Lawrence, Brother. *The Practice of the Presence of God*. Numerous editions.

Maltz, Maxwell. *Psycho-Cybernetics*. New York: Pocket Books, 1969.

Miller, Lisa. *The Awakened Brain: The New Science of Spirituality*. New York: Random House, 2021.

Silva, José. *The Silva Mind Control Method*. New York: Pocket Books, 1978.

Vitale, Joe. *Attract Money Now*. Wimberley, TX: Hypnotic Marketing, 2009. www.AttractMoneyNow.com.

———. *The Attractor Factor: 5 Easy Steps for Creating Wealth (or Anything Else) from the Inside Out.* Hoboken, NJ: John Wiley & Sons, Inc., 2006.

———. *At Zero: The Final Secrets to "Zero Limits," the Quest for Miracles Through Ho'oponopono.* Hoboken, NJ: John Wiley & Sons, Inc., 2013.

———. *The Awakened Millionaire.* Hoboken, NJ: John Wiley & Sons, Inc., 2016.

———. *The Awakening Course.* Hoboken, NJ: John Wiley & Sons, Inc., 2010.

———. *The Fifth Phrase.* New York: G&D Media, 2022.

———. *Karmic Marketing.* New York: G&D Media, 2021.

———. *Life's Missing Instruction Manual.* Hoboken, NJ: John Wiley & Sons, Inc., 2006.

———. *The Miracle: Six Steps to Enlightenment.* Wimberley, TX: Hypnotic Marketing, 2016.

———. *Miracles Manual. 3 vols.* Wimberley, TX: Hypnotic Marketing. http://www.miraclesmanual.com.

———. *The Seven Lost Secrets of Success.* Hoboken, NJ: John Wiley & Sons, Inc., 2011.

———. *There's a Customer Born Every Minute.* Hoboken, NJ: John Wiley & Sons, Inc., 2006.

———. *Unexpected Kindness.* New York: G&D Media, 2024.

BIBLIOGRAPHY

Vitale, Joe, and Dr. Ihaleakala Hew Len. *Zero Limits: The Secret Hawaiian System for Wealth, Health, Peace, and More.* Hoboken, NJ: John Wiley & Sons, Inc., 2007.

Wattles, Wallace. *Financial Success Through Creative Thought or the Science of Getting Rich.* Holyoke, MA: Elizabeth Towne, 1910.

ABOUT THE AUTHOR

Dr. Joe Vitale—once homeless but now a motivating *inspi-rator* known to his millions of fans as "Mr. Fire!"—is the world-renowned author of numerous bestselling books, such as *The Attractor Factor, Zero Limits, Life's Missing Instruc-tion Manual, The Secret Prayer, Attract Money Now* (free at www.AttractMoneyNow.com), *The Awakened Millionaire,*

Karmic Marketing, Hypnotic Writing, and *The Miracle,* to name a few of his popular titles.

A media personality seen on major programs around the world, Dr. Vitale's online television show, *Zero Limits Living,* can be seen at www.ZeroLimitsLivingTV.com, and his podcast can be heard at www.JoeVitalePodcast.com.

According to *Success* magazine, he is considered one of the top fifty most inspiring speakers in the world. He travels around the globe, from Ireland to Russia, to Italy and Poland, sharing his uplifting messages and inspiring stories on stages everywhere.

He starred in the blockbuster movie *The Secret,* as well as more than twenty films. He has recorded many bestselling audio programs, including *The Missing Secret* and *The Zero Point.*

He's considered the world's first self-help singer-songwriter, as seen in *Rolling Stone* magazine, with more than fifteen albums and many of his songs nominated for the Posi Award (considered the Grammys of positive music). His latest album, called *The Great Something,* was dedicated to legendary performer Melissa Etheridge.

Dr. Vitale created Miracles Coaching®, The Awakening Course, The Secret Mirror, Hypnotic Writing, Advanced Ho‘oponopono Certification, and many more life-transforming products and services. He currently lives outside of Austin, Texas, with his love, Lisa Winston, and their puppy, Cabi. His main website is www.MrFire.com.

Follow Dr. Joe Vitale via:

- Instagram: https://www.instagram.com/drjoevitale
- TV Show: www.ZeroLimitsLivingTV.com
- Podcast: www.JoeVitalePodcast.com
- Coaching: www.MiraclesCoaching.com
- X (formerly known as Twitter): https://x.com/mrfire
- Facebook: https://www.facebook.com/drjoevitale
- Blog: http://blog.mrfire.com
- YouTube: https://www.youtube.com/user/JoeMrFire